© 2021 Ngoma Hill

Ngoma Hill
I Didn't Come Here to Tap Dance (A Poetic Memoir)

All rights reserved. No part of this publication may be reproduced, stored in a retrieval system or transmitted in any form or by any means, electronic, mechanical, photocopying, recording or otherwise without the prior permission of the publisher or in accordance with the provisions of the Copyright, Designs and Patents Act 1988 or under the terms of any license permitting limited copying issued by the Copyright Licensing Agency.

**Published by:** Cordell Hill

**Text Design by:** Empress.Poetry1@gmail.com

**Cover Design by:** SoRichGraphix@gmail.com

**Artwork by:** Iyaba Ibo Mandingo

**Back Cover Photo Credit**: Osunyoyin Alake Ifariki

A CIP record for this book is available from the Library of Congress Cataloging-in-Publication Data

**ISBN-13:** 978-0-578-99460-4
**Distributed by:**

Cordell Hill
1845 Adam C. Powell Blvd
Apt. #3D
New York, NY 10026

NGOMA HILL


I DIDN'T COME HERE TO TAP DANCE
(A Poetic Memoir)

# I Didn't Come Here to Tap Dance

Ngoma Hill

# Contents

## *I Didn't Ask to Come Here*

| | |
|---|---|
| I Didn't Ask to Come Here | 2 |
| Where I Come From | 3 |
| Countdown to 65 - Poem 3 | 4 |
| Funny Thing Is | 6 |
| Up South | 9 |
| Until We're Free | 12 |
| I Didn't Come Here to Tap Dance | 14 |

## *The Year Long Back Packing Trip thru Sunny Southeast Asia*

| | |
|---|---|
| Countdown to 65 - Poem 7 | 17 |
| Countdown to 65 - Poem 8 | 19 |
| F.T.A. (Support Our Troops/Bring Them Home) | 21 |
| Real War Stories | 24 |
| Where Were You When the King of Love Was Killed? | 26 |
| Grunt | 28 |

Sister Soldiers     30

After My Year Long Backpacking Trip thru Sunny Southeast Asia     32

They Say There Are No Atheists in Fox Holes     34

The Recruiter     35

### *I'm Gonna Do What the Spirit Says Do*

Searching for Ogun     38

Return to the Source     42

Poem for My Egun     44

Paradigm Shiftin' (Flippin da Script on Myths)     46

New Millennium Dream     49

Mom Believed in Jesus     52

A Poet's Prayer to Obatala     54

Palm Sunday's Ritual     55

Eleri Ipin     57

Countdown to 65 - Poem 13     59

Whose Civilization?     61

They Walk thru Life with Eyes Wide Shut     62

Morning Meditations     64

| | |
|---|---|
| Sitting on the Edge of Tomorrow | 65 |
| Residue on the Altar of Time | 66 |

## *Music Is My Essence*

| | |
|---|---|
| I'm a String Scientist | 68 |
| A Love Story | 69 |
| A Poem in Response to the Question What Kind of Music Do You Play? | 71 |
| Fiddle Me This | 72 |
| String (In Memory of Billy Bang) | 73 |
| Brown Butterfly | 74 |
| We String Scientists | 77 |
| D.W.B. (Didj'n While Black) - A True Story from the Village of Harlem | 78 |
| This Bloody Business Called Music | 80 |
| Jazz Doesn't Live Here Anymore | 82 |
| Music Is My Essence | 84 |

## **All the Blues That's Fit to Read**

| | |
|---|---|
| Why Newspapers Are Becoming Obsolete | 87 |
| Who Killed Orphan Annie? | 88 |
| My Pen's Got a Point | 89 |

| | |
|---|---|
| B4 the End of the World | 90 |
| I Don't Believe God Did This | 92 |
| His Story | 94 |
| Funktastic | 96 |
| Java | 97 |
| Starfuck | 98 |
| Convo with Rod | 100 |
| Bloodstained Handprints on the Wailing Wall (For Palestine) | 102 |
| Opinion of a Fly on the Wall (Trick or Treat) | 104 |
| Sneakaz | 105 |
| The State of Emergency That Nobody Told You About or the Low Down on the Down Low (Conspiracy Theory 101) | 107 |
| Pick Up Whatever You Can Pick Up | 110 |
| On the Day the Pope Died | 114 |
| Uncomfortable Conversations | 117 |
| I'm in a Recovery Program from Western Civilization | 120 |
| Anatomy of a Lynching (Contemporary Sketches of Amerikkka) | 122 |
| Countdown Y2K | 124 |
| Poem for the Absent Minded | 126 |

One Last Poem for Amiri B                             129

Don't Call Me No Poet (This Ain't No Love Song)       131

## *The Corona Chronicles*

The Hood Greets Rona                                  135

Said I Wasn't Gonna Talk About Death                  136

Fear of a Black Planet                                137

Mother Nature Has No Cashapp                          138

Masks (What Will Be Will Be)                          139

This Plandemic Ain't New                              141

SOS on the Nu Titanic                                 142

20/20                                                 144

Breakin' News                                         145

The Scream of Silence                                 146

Things Fall Apart                                     147

In the Absence of Ka-Ching                            149

Aftermath                                             150

The Real Amerikkka                                    152

The House Is on Fyah                                  153

Pestilence                            155

Pass/Past/Puff                        157

E.P.K.

## Livication

Livicated to Amiri Baraka, Mikey Smith, Victor Jara, Louis Reyes Rivera, Zannette Lewis, and all the Word Warriors that dared to use words as their weapon.

# Acknowledgements

Shoutout and thanks to Dr. Helena Lewis, Leah Jackson, and James Ellerbe who encouraged me to publish this book.

Thanks to Bill Holmes for editing.

Thanks to Osunyoyin Alake Ifariki for inspiration; to the fam - Teng, Marcus, Trina, David, Beth, and Jaribu.

Thanks to Bruce Bozeman for opening the door to my political consciousness.

Thanks to all my friends and comrades in the struggle for a better life.

# Foreword

*(For Baba Ngoma Osayemi Ifatunmise)*

He is a griot,
Reincarnated here,
in the perfect time and place.
Because you need to hear him.
His ancestral ears remembered
The Kontigi, the Ngoni African
string instruments.
Unable to find them he took a new wife,
the violin.
Years passed before he was able to make
her sing the old ways,
in a new voice.
But he did.
Married her,
worked with her,
mastered her...

The realm of the griots heard their
favored son,
bestowed their blessings,
gave him a pen and papyrus
and released the word
from his tongue,
full of afose and fire it burned
down illusions, lies, and trickery.
His words awakened thought,
consciousness, and spiritual thirst.
He exposed the chicanery of those

who had stolen your power, your resources, your mind,
and your soul.
He gave it back to you,
if you are willing
to take possession of it.

In the world of spirit and shadow the ancestors nodded
affirmation in recognition of his genius.
Past generations spoke their messages thru his lips,
Spoke in history.
Spoke in prophecy.
Spoke in the Now.
They gave him more instruments,
woke up the improvisation of the
magical spirit in his psyche and fingers.
Called him Ngoma,
meaning music,
meaning drum,
meaning spiritual possession when dancing to that drum.
Set him on the path they scripted long before his birth.
His breath cried for the vast ancient
task of creation and the Yidaki appeared
resonant in his possession.
Each encounter re-sounding the world into being,
opening up secret spiritual centers in
his being, in his listeners lives.
The hallowed ones, silent, omnipresent and intent, covered
him in ase on his journey,
Ogun wrapped him in palm fronds,
Elegba opened the path back to Africa,
Obatala pushed patience in practice
paving longer roads of creativity,

Ifa started his life over again.
By their authority and the mission of his destiny,
he says what you don't want to hear,
tells you what you need to know,
reminds you of where you come from
and where truth says you need to go,
on a cloud of music and a lightning strike voice
to carve it deep into your once sleeping spirit.
Because that's what Soul does,
because that's what Soul is...
Baba Ngoma Osayemi Ifatumise.
That is what Soul sounds like.

Copyright © Osunyoyin Alake April 2014.

I Didn't Come Here to Tap Dance (A Poetic Memoir)

# *I Didn't Ask to Come Here*

## I Didn't Ask to Come Here

I didn't ask to come here
I was kidnapped
tied up tied down
to the bottom of a slave ship
transported like cattle
I didn't ask to come here
feel the slavers lash forever
ask Rodney King, Phillip Pannell,
and Grandmother Eleanor Bumpurs
I didn't ask to come here
nobody asked if I wanted to be a citizen
I didn't hi-jack a boat
to come to these shores
to lose my name, my religion,
my ancestors, my land, my mind
I didn't ask to integrate nor assimilate
no more auction block for me
I didn't ask to be Amerikkkan
at least not the ones that killed Vietnamese babies,
spread man made dis-eases,
spilled blood and guts
in the name of the cross, the lash, and the gun,
stole the Indians land, leveled the Holy Land
-and before I'd be a slave
I'd be buried in my grave-
I just want to be accepted
in the human race
with peace, love, justice, and equality.

## Where I Come From

I come from back of the bus
and colored water fountains
I come from segregated toilets
and no niggas or dogs allowed
I come from segregated and unequal schools
with hand me down books
I come from sit up in the balcony
I come from "You can't buy a house in this neighborhood!"
I come from "You can't eat at this lunch counter!"
I come from "Go round the back to get your food!"
I come from picket lines, bus boycotts, and fire hoses
I come from freedom rides, freedom songs, and jail cells
I come from we've been buked and we've been scorned
I come from we shall overcome
I come from Black Fist raised high
Little Bobby Hutton, Fred Hampton, and George Jackson
I come from street fightin' and rebellion
San Quentin and Attica
Black Panthers, Young Lords, and Free Breakfast Programs
I come from runaway slaves
I come from Amiri Baraka, Simba Wachanga, and Watu Wazuri
I come from pour libations on ancestors' graves
I come from the struggle to be free,
to be free, to be free.

## Countdown to 65 - Poem 3

As a child coming up below the Mason Dixon line
I was kind of oblivious to white folk
there were none in my neighborhood
and we didn't have a car
sometimes we'd sit at the back of the bus to go downtown
but the lunch counters and changing rooms
were unavailable to us coloreds
besides my aunts were cooks and waitresses
for the genteel
they could rock some pots and pans
my grandma had 16 children and there was always food to eat
my grandfather worked on the railroad
when A. Philip Randolph organized
The Brotherhood of Sleeping Car Porters
I was down with Black Power
before Stokely (as we called him back then)
raised his fist and voice at Howard U
the block boys called it How Weird but that's another bop.
At VSC the administration wouldn't allow him
an auditorium to speak so we seized the steps at Va. Hall
encouraged by a speech that made us ponder
about why Black men should fight white men's wars
some of us still grapple with that question
after all the Vietnamese never called us nigga
the draft was in full effect
and Muhammad Ali set the example
H. Rap Brown told us to "Burn, Baby, Burn,"
our consciousness was evolving
from Negroes to Black to Afrikans.

There was nothing peaceful about the movement for Civil rights,
Klansmen and burning crosses owned the night.
Later I met one of the Deacons for Defense *
it was then that the struggle made more sense

Check out:
* http://en.wikipedia.org/wiki/Deacons_for_Defense_and_Justice

## Funny Thing Is

I never thought much about
growing old
didn't realize that I was
until
in a group discussion with young poets
I mentioned that I went to High School and college
in the Jim Crow South
before integration
we actually had teachers that cared
we didn't wear jeans to school
it just wasn't allowed
we never thought that it was uncool
in fact we birthed the cool
male teachers wore suits and ties
women teachers wore skirts and dresses
you could tell the teachers from the students
and people dressed up when they went to church
in fact church was like a fashion show
everyone wore their best
I never argued with dad about
whether or not I could use the car
we didn't have a car
in fact I remember before Rosa Parks
we rode in the back of the bus
we debated much more serious issues
like integrating schools
and the fact that I never really wanted to go to school
with white people
it wasn't that I disliked them
it's just that all of my friends were Black
and that they were foreign to me
none lived in my neighborhood
going in their neighborhood could get your ass kicked
and vice versa

besides my H.S. marching band was the best in the state
we didn't play Souza
we rocked the hits like "Hit the Road Jack"
and danced the Wobble and the Jerk.
I grew up on Saturday night doo wop
and Sunday morning gospel
I learned harmony underneath the streetlights
we sang songs like "In the Still of the Night"
after graduation we didn't try to dodge the draft
it would have been an embarrassment to the family
besides my mom worked as a secretary for the government
it was one of the better jobs for colored people
although the water fountains and restrooms were still segregated
I walked picket lines in the 60's
my dad was a plaintiff in the Brown vs. Board of Education suit
he got fired from his job for it
we integrated theaters, stores,
lunch counters, and churches too
some white kids joined but they were mostly into peace and love
we grew into Black Power:
Stokely Carmichael became Kwame Toure,
Leroi Jones became Imamu Amiri Baraka,
I became Ngoma.
I was an infantryman in Vietnam
long before Hip Hop
we wore Afros and Converse
before Adidas Shell Tops
I told you me and Miles we birthed the cool
after Nam heroin was king
Panthers and Simbas owned the night
until Cointelpro

Fred Hampton and Bobby Hutton
lay in their graves
soldiers coming home in body bags…
funny thing is
I never thought I'd live long enough
to grow old.

# Up South

She says
write a poem about
being a poet from New York
I'm thinking hmmmmm,
that could be hard.
See to begin with
I've lived here since '79
but I'm not from New York
I'm from Richmond, VA
the capitol of the Confederacy
I followed the North Star
like a run-a-way slave searching for freedom
trying to get away from picket lines
and klan signs
only to find
ku klux killer kops
hiding behind badges instead of sheets.
Now, don't get me wrong
I love New York
during my college days all of my boys bit from the Big Apple
I hung out with them cause they were the coolest
but they're all gone now
so I pour a sip for Lou Wheeler and Leslie Scott
I'd take my little money from a summer job at Minisink
to buy Italian knits, sharkskin pants,
and playboy shoes with the thick rubber souls
from McCreedy and Schrieber
I wouldn't tell anyone where I was really from
all the flyest girls liked brothers from New York
and I wanted to be cool like that.
My boys introduced me to Black Power, Black Muslims,
Black Nationalist, Black Panthers,

and Black Poetry
Imamu Amiri Baraka (as he was called then)
Haki Madhubuti a.k.a. Don L. Lee,
Carolyn Rogers, Askia Muhammad Toure, and
The Last Poets -
of course with the exception of some of the Last
Poets,
none of them were from New York anyway -
but it didn't matter to me
I just wanted to be like them
I'd never heard talk like that before -
I was hooked
and poetry was my drug of choice
Malcolm's murder
triggered the Black Arts Movement
the seed was planted
watered, and nurtured at all the poetry spots
The Spirit House in Newark, The East and Uhuru
Sasa Shule in Brooklyn,
The African Poetry Theater in Queens, and The
National Black Theater
in Harlem
but then, you wanted to know about the poetry
thing is, I never called myself a poet,
djeli or griot might be a better description
since I rock anything with a string plus I can sing
some call me Dr. Rocka Fiddle
the God-Father of spoken word
you'd better ask somebody if you haven't heard
actually I write a lot too
you might say I'm just a pissed off brother with a pen
one of my friends reminded me
Amerikkka is a place where the past always looks like
the future
but these twisted I want to be hip hoppers
and ku klux killer kops

think niggas come in all colors
so I still do protests and die ins
cause in this atmosphere
I Can't Breathe
and New York just seems like
Up South to me.

## Until We're Free

Hadn't talked to her in awhile
she's near Lemiert Park
she says
you still doing that poetry and music thing
I figured you would have retired by now
lotta folk we know just gave up on slingin rocks at
Goliath
the kids all wear white t-shirts to the funeral
tribal warfare block by block
that they moms pay rent for
gang warfare is the order of the day
from the microcosm of street gangs
fighting for a piece of the rock
to the Empire's Battalions filling their bank accounts
salesman of war suck the blood of the poor
immigrant children in concentration camps
ghetto children in for profit foster care
the largest prison industrial complex on the planet
like global holocaust
from micro to maximum
a bad dream reality nightmare
middle passage reincarnated
slave trade in Libya
the world's for sale to the highest bidder
bid em in bid em in
there's a sale on Black babies by the pound
on the black market
Obomber Blacklash Blues
reconstruction revisited
nobody tell you?  Planned Parenthood is genocide
you could get arrested breathing while Black
castrated and hanged in Nuyo Dixie
anyplace south of Canada
the real terrorist

burn Tiki torches in Charlottesville
use niggas for target practice after dark
heat marshmallows in the flames of
cross burnings at klan rallies
still deny clean water in Ferguson
so you ask
you still doing that poetry and music thing
well, you betta ask somebody
obviously no one told you
I'll be doing this
until we're free.

## I Didn't Come Here to Tap Dance

I didn't come here to tap dance!
I was born in the 7th month
two months early
in a rush to
shine my light on darkness
born in water with fire on my tongue
always had a lot to say
it's true I fiddle around some
but I didn't come here to tap dance.
You could call me a stripper
cause I strip the covers off of bullshit
born in the 7th month
two months early
I first protested
when the doctor smacked me on the ass
haven't had much trust for them since
I'm the question mark
the teacher didn't have the answer to,
I'm the poet professors warned you about
a past/present/future thought
to make you think about tomorrow
but all time is now
and yesterday was never promised
all words matter.
I was born in the 7th month
two months early
fully armed with a machine gun mouth
I circular breath Yidaki sound but
I didn't come here to tap dance!
A student of struggle
with a doctorate in resistance
word/sound/power is my weapon

still strong at three quarters of a century
my music opens chakras
my hands invoke reiki
I am a healing force in the universe
a light worker
in a quest to resolve contradictions
I was born in the 7th month
two months early
and I didn't here come to tap dance!
Obatala watches over me,
Esu and Ogun protect me,
Osun is my mother,
Egun speaks thru me,
I inhale darkness and exhale light
I was born in the 7th month
two months early
and I did not come here to tap dance,
so don't ask questions
that you really don't want answers to
unless you're prepared for evolution
you may not like the resolution.
I didn't come here to tap dance!

# ***The Year Long Back Packing Trip thru Sunny Southeast Asia***

# Countdown to 65 - Poem 7

It was somewhere around December 23$^{rd}$ of 1967
when the postman delivered the mail
and believe me it was no Cashmas card
instead the letter said
"Greetings from Uncle Sam!"
needless to say I was quite disturbed
I had just gotten married and moved into a new apartment
besides that I didn't have any uncles named Sam
for those of you too young to know
it was a notice from the draft
seems like my new year
was starting out pretty screwed up
with orders to report for duty
in the U.S. Army.
Draft resistance wasn't too popular
for Black folk,
Canada was out of the question
none of my dad's high fallutin' friends
had a solution to relieve my destitution
so I soon found myself on a train
headed to Ft. Gordon
in Augusta, GA,
the home of James Brown
and you best believe
no one gave a damn that we sang
"Say It Loud (I'm Black and I'm Proud)"
Augusta was one step past slavery
the sidewalks rolled up at 1800 hours
although it took a while before we got passes to check it out.
On Sunday there was one black and white TV in the barracks
that only broadcast church service

once we donned army greens and had our heads shaved
everyone was anonymous before name tags
there was a group of Puerto Ricans fresh off the boat
I'm still in a quandry about what they were doing there
because Puerto Rico was yet to be a U.S. state
and none of them spoke a word of English
when the sergeant barked at them in English
they'd respond with a "No comprende!"
this got them out of doing any work for two days
so I decided to join them responding "No comprende!" when spoken to
this worked fine until we were assigned to a Spanish speaking sergeant
thus began my stint in Uncle Sam's Army
the sign on the entrance gate said INFANTRY – FOLLOW ME
I knew it was going to be a long two years
being pissed off and rather defiant
I was always looking for ways not to follow orders
the only stripes I wanted were pinstripes
and dying for a country where I had no civil rights
was not on my agenda.

## Countdown to 65 - Poem 8

It was at least 90 degrees
humidity thick enough to cut with a chain saw
when I stepped off the plane in Cam Rahn Bay
I started to look around for the devil
cause I was damn sure this was hell
and we had missed our stop
the air quality was thick with the smell
of diesel oil and shit
the terrain was so sandy
that there were boardwalk type sidewalks
from building to building
this was home near the beach for about a week
It was just after the Tet Offensive
the 1st Cav and 101st Airborne
had just had their asses kicked
fighting hand to hand when the NVA over ran
the bunker complex
the B-52's had dropped their loads
and we were going to check out the damage
ammo loaded and ruck sacked
we packed into helicopters
headed for a mountain top near Dakto called Mile High
dug bunkers and filled sandbags
'neath a blazing sun
the army was the first institution
I was a part of that was integrated
but that theory was highly overrated
Blacks socialized with Blacks
and whites with white
the only time there was unity
was in a fire fight
but everyone looked the same
in the dark of night

otherwise the brothers smoked good Cambodian red ganja
while the rednecks drank Jack
it was a year or so before G.I's got hooked
smoking smack
although we were at war we still partied hard
in this business there was need for a mental escape
the stakes were high and there weren't many breaks
we were fighting a war within a war
if you were unpopular
you might get fragged
a rosary might not save you from a body bag
some decorated their helmets with the sign of the cross
I figured out death might be coming soon
on my helmet was a prayer to Ogun
from then on I felt protected
no monument to my memory
need be erected.

# F.T.A. (Support Our Troops/Bring Them Home)

My lover told me
that in past lives
I must have been Abraxas
but the docs said it was
post-traumatic stress disorder
so I self-medicated with mushrooms and meth
trying to figure out the mess inside my head
now if you can handle it
we'll take a trip inside
put on your safety belt
if you want to take this ride
from the sidewalks of Virginia
to Pleiku's mountainsides
it was back in '68
after the time of Tet
when I crossed the burning sands
of Cam Ranh Bay
where the stench of burning shit and diesel oil
permeated the air
you could tell I was a FNG by the cut of my hair
while short time screaming eagles and 1st Cav guys
with stubbled beards
babbled endless stories about how Tet had been
with the Mighty Vietcong overran bunker complexes
and fought them hand to hand
or how the 4th Div got wiped out
in the Valley of Plei Trap
between Cambodia and Vietnam
Where the VC tied themselves in the trees
and those damn AK47's
had us on our hands and knees praying there was a God in heaven
low crawling thru rice paddies full of water buffalo shit

crawling underground as a tunnel rat
finding huge bunkers 50 feet of concrete overhead
when we found ourselves surrounded,
many wounded many dead.
Now, there up on a hillside
in a shack stretched out on racks
we identified the bodies
that won't be coming back
thru blood sweat and mayhem
we manage to survive
one day you're in the mountains
the next day in the streets
trying to become accustomed to concrete beneath
your feet
trying to collect your benefits in this land of
opportunity
welcome home soldier
you'll surely need a friend
cause you only return to where the cycle began
where you joined the military cause you got drafted
or you couldn't find a job
the recruitment office in the ghetto
said be all that you can be
now you're homeless and suffering
back from overseas
where statistics of homeless vets
add up to 300,000
where disability claims could take a few years
and while you get worst
it's easy for a soldier to die first
lost in a system waiting list 127,000
in New York alone and the numbers with be mounting
coming home from Iraq and Afghanistan
plus the walking dead from the conflict in Vietnam
waiting on Section 8 and medical care
standing in line for welfare

after fighting on the front line for democracy
angry, scared, broke, divorced, depressed
hostile, resentful, suicidal, and stressed
self-medicated to relieve the stress
from the military to filthy shelters or the slums
sleeping on subways
thought of as bums
in this home of the brave
this land of the free.
"I didn't fail my country, my country failed me"

P.S. F.T.A. means Fuck the Army

## Real War Stories

I spent the years '68 and '69
backpacking thru sunny Southeast Asia
smoking the best Cambodian Red
and sleeping with the stars as my canopy
loaded for bear
I could kill anything walking
I sipped strawberry wine from Dakto
packed in red mail bags from Pleiku
humped from chopper pads
where helicopter blades
fanned the stench of burning shit and diesel oil in the air.
I slept on mountain sides so steep
you had to dig a shelf in mother earth to keep from rolling down the hillside
drank crystal meth and listened to the stars all night.
Montagnard drums kept me company
between mortar fire
mother earth became my lover
as we hugged her for safety
submitting to her rhythm
as tracer rounds filled up the darkness,
it's strange, the power that you feel
when everyone is armed
sad to think it's necessary
take a ride with me on a chopper
feet dangling out the doors
swooping above the trees
flying like a bird
makes you think you're God
til the V.C. shoots you down
with an AK47
fill your pipe with morning dew
with a pinch of opium

makes breakfast taste better
meatballs and beans cooked over C4
stolen from a Claymore mine
crackers, canned peaches, and peanut butter
to start the day
a cold beer buried in the ground overnight
a Kool cigarette sent from home
breakfast of champions
it's one hundred degrees in the
shade of banana trees
the grass in An Khe is manicured by water buffalo
leaving clops of shit to maneuver around
the pimps bring women, weed, whiskey,
bangles, and anything you can imagine
on the back of their mopeds
ancient versus future
ice cold Coca-Cola - one dollah.

## Where Were You When the King of Love Was Killed?

April 4,1968:
the trigger pulled, the bullet cried at 6:01,
heartbeat ceased at 7:05.
Lorraine was the woman scorned,
it was Bluff City
the place that Elvis ruined,
St. Joseph did not, could not save him
the D'evil was not bluffing
the digits were against him
the math total equaled six
the number for sacrifice,
the number for caring,
the number for healing,
the number for teaching others,
the number for protection,
but he left his Juju home
peace and harmony forsake him
conspiracy completed
the bullet was no love letter
destiny with his appointment
to protest inequality incinerated
garbage men and their mothers
mourned with the rest of the world
a young draftee
I was in the barracks
looking at my reflection
in newly spit shined boots
pondering how soon I might get sent to 'Nam
when the news broke on the radio
a redneck muttered under his breath
"Good, the nigga's dead!"
it was at Ft Pricks a.k.a Ft Dix
when the lights went out

and the riot started
I don't remember how long it took
for the MPs to break it up
the next day's training
was how to quell mob violence
I stood firm with the brothers who resisted
and decided not to go.

## Grunt

I keep getting compliments on this picture
and I keep asking why
funny thing is how old photos lie
like this one
or how everybody's got their own idea
of what was really going on
like we should be proud
to protect our country
while struggling for human rights
I never saw it that way
I was drafted, I didn't volunteer,
it wasn't my idea to go a strange land
hunt down the locals and kill them
after all the whole deal was a lie
there never was a threat to U.S. soil
only diamonds, opium, and oil
to protect
most G.I.s never knew why.
Here's the real picture:
Tet was over
we'd already lost the war
most of the time we spent
looking for the mighty NVA.
but they'd already hit and run
as we sat on fire bases in the mountains of Pleiku
Shorty from Carolina singing "(Sittin On) The Dock of the Bay"
til the night he got hit by a shrapnel and med evaced away
guarding ghosts in bunkers
that the V.C. with an AK and a bowl of rice had overrun
riding dragons wearing sandals
made of rubber tires

by Firestone
we smoked gold from Cambodia
with a sip of strawberry wine
waiting for the monsoon to stop
to run search and destroy patrols
checking out bomb craters
where the 1st Cav fought hand to hand
thinking fat Sam had the upper hand
but I wasn't down with all that
follow me, I'm infantry jive
I was with the brothers that resisted and stayed alive
we organized the write in vote for Dick Gregory's
Peace and Freedom Party
shared Black Panther papers and *Muhammad Speaks*
so our spirit could survive
poured libations to Ogun
always united raising the Black fist
listening to Curtis sing "Keep On Pushing"
Marvin crooning "What's Going On?"
giving dap and flipping scripts
giving patriotism a twist
we knew who the real enemy was
they never called us nigger.

## Sister Soldiers

Sister soldiers
mothers' daughters
serving their time on the front line
pledged allegiance to blood spattered banners
breed more ghost than previous battles
due to economic drafts and lying ads
who tell them to be all that they can be
so they sign in blood on the dotted line
blood being the perfect symbol
surrendering to the eagle
to be prey like fresh meat to a beast
emerging from their battle buddy
when you realize your only friend
is your gun and knife
your male compatriots
with whom you stand and fight
see you as a ho, a bitch, or a dyke
cause real women aint spozed to fight
so when you report them
you're accused of lies
and the brass tries to disguise the truth
like it's your fault
so you're less afraid of mortar rounds
than the fellas you eat with each day
and you stay strapped
just to go to the latrine or to pray
they say you're just eye candy
replacing the prostitutes in Vietnam
but you're a machine gunner
with two purple hearts
on a second tour
in a combat zone
being abused and disrespected
a long way from home

now I'm sure you want to know why this story
is being told by a man
the answer is simple
because I care
and I can.

P.S. In today's U.S. Army 30% of women have been raped, 71% physically assaulted and 90% sexually harassed

## After My Year Long Backpacking Trip Thru Sunny Southeast Asia

Walking on concrete seemed really strange
trying to sleep in a bed was weird too
it seemed like it was too soft
it was still hot in Virginia is September
so at least I wasn't shocked by the weather
but buses backfiring had me wanting to duck for cover
Labor Day fireworks didn't help much either
I wasn't working yet so with time on my hands
wooded parks were quite comforting
my boys had supplied me with a steady diet of revolutionary literature
and the camaraderie of brothers in 'Nam
had me thinking a revolution was about to jump off
after all the Last Poets and Black Panthers were all in the news
J. Edgar Whoever had declared them dangerous
red, black, and green buttons and necklaces with Black fists
were popular too
I came back mad as hell with an itchy trigger finger
ready for the shit to jump off
Cambodian red and tabs of good acid comforted me
but otherwise didn't help the problem either
nobody told me I was suffering from PTSD
there was no debriefing
had me thinking there was some real Black Unity back in the world
my marriage was going to shit
paranoia had me thinking everyone was an agent
after attending a Panther rally I learned the feds were questioning my friends
the idiots paid me a visit
asked my opinion on revolution

like I'd really tell them
I told them all Black People should
move back to Africa
having survived Pleiku and the Tet Offensive
I set out to make up for all the nookie I had missed
good poon tang is life affirming
and I needed to check daily to see if I was still alive
trust was a bit hard to come by
so I set out to find people of like minds
most of the homies were strung out partying
scag was taking over the neighborhood
even the offspring of the Black bourgeoisie nodded
the Talented Tenth mainlined
not liking needles I dodged the doogie bullet
everybody else was strung out on Jesus
I was searching for Ogun
but this was the late '60's in the Black Belt South
and he was hiding out not to be found
I thought about checking out the N.O.I.
but I was too cool for that
I rocked bell bottom hip huggers
and a big Afro
bow ties and bean pie just didn't satisfy
my sense of style
packed up my VW Bug
snuck off to Newark in the middle of the night
looking for the revolution.

## They Say There Are No Atheists in Fox Holes

Perhaps only the Devil wages war
but you won't see him fighting one
instead he sends your children
misguided and misunderstood
thinking that the battle will give them peace
at least that's what the leaders say
obviously they've never been in fox holes
I never trusted presidents
they always seem to get away with murder
sometimes it is protracted
slow death on the killing ground
the struggle to survive the aftermath of chaos
tattooed on your mind
matching the praying hands
on your shoulder
begging protection from the enemy
have you ever seen the scars of war
a stump dangling from a hospital gown
where a leg used to be
a prosthetic hand to sign the check
that never comes
waiting for that job you can no longer do
from a wheelchair
pain and disillusion a constant companion
begging spare change your occupation
searching for salvation
from your fox hole.

## The Recruiter

I used to have a handle on life, but then it broke,
now that the heat is on
I gotta wear more sunblock
I started to rob a bank
until I realized that Wall Street already did that
it's really a problem
since I'm addicted to eating
and the fast food joints are floating belly up
like dead water bugs after the real kill
I started to join the Army
but got turned down when they realized
that I could read the small print
it seems they couldn't handle a black man with a worldview
since critical thought is not allowed
they only wanted yes men
I didn't come with instructions
there's no program to be downloaded
it's hard to make a soldier
out of someone whose religion is peace
the recruiter said that I should get a hair cut
I said there was a problem I had cool hair
but there were no cool barbers
he asked if I were gay
I told him no but I'd fallen on hard times
and for cash he could suck my johnson
he said he would but was afraid that he'd
be dishonorably discharged
he was only there for benefits
he'd done two tours in Iraq
his brain was suffering depleted uranium rot
he realized he couldn't spend
the medals that he got
and the pawn shop wasn't offering much

for a purple heart
so he re-upped to sell dreams
that turn to nightmares to the dispossessed
though he knew that it was bad karma
and his soul could never rest
said his emotions
stepped on a landmine
but the medics sewed him up
and said that he'd be fine
they didn't tell him that
to the truth he'd be forever blind
or that his acquired condition
would destroy his mind
so now he struggles with demon contradictions
a walking time bomb with twisted convictions.

# I'm Gonna Do What the Spirit Says Do

# Searching for Ogun
# (An Autobiographical War Story at Home and Abroad)

I met Ogun
between the pages of a book
near a rice paddy outside of Pleiku
hanging out with Boukman, Mackandall, Dessalines,
and Celestine
explaining how they
kicked Napoleon's ass at Port au Prince
I figured there was something to it
so I wrote OGUN FERRAILLE BE WITH ME
on the band to my steel pot helmet
the Cambodian red was good and the opium
put me in another place and kept my head on straight
the crystal meth was great for mountain climbing
especially blazing trails thru the Central Highlands
where no man walked before.
My man Rusty from B-More rocked an M79 like it was
automatic
his specialty was duck, dive, roll, and fire,
he could put a grenade on a gnat's ass half a mile
away.
The Ole Man from Houston
had a thing for AK47s
said the M-16s weren't worth shit
but you could pull an AK out of the mud and still fire it.
I was the fucking new guy
me and machine guns were lovers
my side man was Jim
from Gulfport, Mississippi
a big dude

he would lug four or five hundred rounds of ammo at a time
machine gunners need to have a death wish
a tracer every fifth round was a guarantee
you needed to be like Muhammad Ali
stick and move, stick and move!
I burned out a barrel in the mountains near Cambodia
it was the night Shorty's legs got blown off
we really missed him and his
singing "(Sittin On) The Dock of the Bay"
when we hung out in the bunkers during monsoon
drinking strawberry wine and puff puff passing
to Otis Redding and Sam Cooke.
Flea survived 10 rounds
got patched up and came back to the field
ringing wet in an overcoat he only weighed about 100 lbs
he was a crazy white boy who had been a screaming eagle
I figured only fools jump out of perfectly good airplanes
he re-upped for another tour
I figured he just drank too much rot gut Jack Daniels and Santori
by then I was a short timer
just trying to survive to catch that last ride
on the freedom bird
back home
hanging heavy with the brothers
we all thought things back in the world would be different
brothers stuck together like glue in Nam
we really had no business fucking with the mighty Viet Cong
and we all thought there'd be some real Black Unity

when we returned
but shit was still fucked up
and heroin was taking over the hood
even doctors and lawyer's kids were strung out
everybody wanted to be Supa Fly
I wasn't into needles
so I let it all pass by
since I'd pledged to the Most High
to be a warrior for my people
I came home looking for Black Panthers
I figured with my experience my skills would be needed
they were mostly in exile getting busted or killed
I was still rolling with Ogun
though I didn't know where to find him
I felt I was protected
ended up looking for him in Newark
but found Baraka and Kawaida
the poetry was good
but I figured just seven principles wasn't cuttin it
spent a month or so in Shanghai, Beijing, and Nanjing
checked out Chairman Mao but we needed a Black thing
realized we couldn't make revolution like he did
our march to freedom would be harder and long
spent over a decade doing Serious Bizness
singing contemporary freedom songs
traveling across the U.S.A.,
Europe, and Africa, too,
trying to figure out what my people need to do
sang for a million people in Central Park
for nuclear disarmament
sang for workers rallies
in Madison Square Garden
sang for rallies at Sydenham

but they closed it down they didn't give a damn
so I decided to continue my search
figured I wouldn't find Ogun in church
so I checked a thousand poetry spots
from New York to Portland to Connecticut
followed drum circles from town to town
trying to see if the Gods of Africa could be found
ran a New Age Fair and got a lot of readings
from readers who told me I should be reading them
finally found a sister that opened the door
led me to the mat of the Babalawo
who told me that for every thing
there was a time and a reason
I'd been searching for Ogun
but Obatala found me
seems like this was the place,
the time and the season
the Odu shared to me destiny's reason
this path is about much more
than sacrifice and blood
it's ultimately
about Oludumare's Love
by Obatala I had been chosen.

## Return to the Source

Esu opened the way,
Ogun cleared the path,
the Egungun sent me
back to the source
back to the root
instead of the branch
27 Babalawos in Ibadan,
Iyanifa to bring balance
Osun's River thru Osogbo
the Holy City of Ile Ife
Yorubaland
tin roof city
overflowing with oil and poverty
rich in spirit and mystery
women balancing lives on their heads
endless speeding motor bikes
overcrowded trucks and minivans
highways flooded with peddlers
who bring anything you can ask for
to the window of your car
corrupt government officials
crooked cops with AK47s hustling naira
the hypnotic sway of lapas
the alarm clock of roosters
the beauty of Ebony African people
defying Cosmopolitan's false standards
tribal scars
asking whose civilization
and what would Webster know anyway
as the veil was lifted to the initiated
secrets written in binary codes
supreme mathematics
in opele and cowrie shells
ancient rhythms

passed from hand to heartbeat
destiny revealed in DNA
each day bringing
lessons to be learned
in this school of life.

## Poem for my Egun

For Pauline and James,
Carrie and Linwood,
Celestine and Herman,
for nameless egungun
lost in the Middle Passage
strange fruit from Dixie trees
memory whiplashed into abandonment
in the name of Jesus
you will never be forgotten
pickers of tobacco and cotton
ditch diggers, gardeners, field hands, and brick layers,
carpenters and dishwashers,
waiters and chamber maids,
hospital orderlies and workers with no unions
victims of 21st Century slavery
for the homeless, the hungry, and the dispossessed
begging on subways,
sleeping on sidewalks
chained and locked up
for New Afrikan Freedom Fighters
locked down behind the wall
never to see the light of day
for the down pressed with no redress
for the djeli and the griot
the invisible ones
for the Sons and Daughters of Africa,
Haiti, Cuba, Brazil, Puerto Rico, the Americas,
and every port the slave ships landed
fear not
I chant this incantation for you:
Oh, Esu, Obatala, Osun, Ifa, Shango
Ogun, Oya, Yemoja, and Elegba
please carry these prayers to Oludumare
we bring snail and she goat

pigeons, rooster, guinea fowl, yam
palm oil, sugar cane, lamb and rum
never forgetting where we've come from
we bring catfish, honey, salt,
bitter kola, shea butter, and gin,
we fling pennies into the wind,
we pray this oppression will end,
we come to take a stand and free the land,
united and without fear we come to take back what is ours
we come for the future
we won't forget the past
there's a trail of bones in the Atlantic deep
we come
demanding retribution
for Ifa never sleeps.

## Paradigm Shiftin' (Flippin da Script on Myths)

I am, I am, I am,
I am the original man.
I was a run-a-way slave,
I was here before time,
time ain't real no how
just something capitalist made up
to control y'all
I can't be controlled
I am that dread head nigga
your mama said to watch out for
niggas were multicultural then
I was here before race
race was just something conquerors used
to divide us
I was here before Adam
Adam was gay and didn't even like apples
Eve was a homegirl
I was the dude next door
we used to throw barbeques in the garden of Eden
brothers had to bring a bottle of wine, a six pack, or a blunt to get in
sister could get in for free
the ascended masters were my posse
me and Cleopatra used to do the wild thing
underneath the steps of the pyramids
me and this poet named Saul
used to sunbathe on the banks of the Nile
me, Rah, Ptah, Osiris and Ma'at
had this bad assed band
we'd jam down by the Sphinx on Saturday nite
on Fridays we'd party in Kush
on long weekends we'd hangout with Krishna
we'd cruise along the banks of the Ganges

on our elephants
me and Buddha were buddies
we'd go to Ile Ife for vacations
hang out with the Orishas,
Yemoja, Obatala, Ogun, and them
the Bible was the first National Enquirer
King James was the editor
I met that brother Jesus
he was a real Black man
young dude
dropped out of school early
could do a mean miracle
changing water to wine and what not
did a mean mean fish fry, too
I was there when he was killed
it was a Judeo-Roman conspiracy
he was a political prisoner
we had a Free Jesus rally
still got my button too
didn't work though
they killed him anyway
should have had Johnnie Cochran for a lawyer
me and Luke made sandals the latest rage
I gave Gabriel trumpet lessons
he could play a mean assed blues
I promised Mary I'd keep her secret
you know she wasn't no virgin
just something she made up
so she could get a welfare check
since Joseph was an absentee father
I thought you figured that out by now
must I tell you everything
look, Jesus told me I could be God
just before he died
I didn't want the responsibility though
I knew all them crazy zealots would be

killing peace makers and saying he told them to do it
I didn't want all that blood and shit on my conscience
I used to slang rocks
no, no, not cocaine;
crystals, amethyst, tigers eyes, turquoise, onyx,
and blue lapis
I was a prophet before it was profitable
thought about getting a psychic hot line
but I couldn't get an 800 number
I was here before language
before you had to worry about people lying
everything was the truth then
I was here before negativity
life was simple then
I was here before fear
I was here before want and need and greed
and war and shame and blame
I was here before darkness
I am the light
I've come to show you the way
follow me
I am truth
I am eternal peace
all we need is love
all we need is love
all we need is love
I am, I am, I am
I and I, I and I, I and I
Jah – Rastafari.

## New Millennium Dream

I snort wheatgrass juice for breakfast
it opens my third eye to the Most High
telling me not to use my stomach as a cemetery
for dead animals
I party with 40s of carrot juice,
ginger, and beets -
helps my tantric love last.
I smoke blunts of poetry
shifts my paradigm
helps me rhyme on time in time
if there is time
I question it
but then
I question everything
it's this telepathy
perhaps you've heard of me
I communicate with trees
they tell me gossip
their roots run deep
to the center of the universe
I open chakras, too,
I use my didgeridoo
for cultural healing
when I play for you
these similes and metaphors
open the doors to your mind that was shut
that's why we're in such a rut
but I channel knowledge from the
kingdom of King Tut
I was a citizen of Atlantis in a past life
that's why I swim thru this illusion
that you think of as life
this one of pain and strife
where you'll be imprisoned

for eternity
until your mind breaks free
and you can really see
things can change when you question authority
like the elimination of reincarnation
in 325 AD
I have no use for a compass
I read the earth's blueprint
don't believe in owning land
or paying landlord's rent
I always give praise to the seven directions
I know that the soul is an act of perfection
we're all made in the image of God
but God has no body
so I study the travel of the soul
it never grows old at least not the way
that you think of as old
for soul is eternal
never ending
the kingdom of Heaven is within
there are spirits seen and unseen
spirits known and unknown
singing life is full of riddles
that only the dead can answer
if you listen you can hear them
in the echoes of the wind
chanting siren sounds
from the place that time began
there goes that word again
I believe in all things as opposed to those who believe
in nothing
I am the center of the crossroads that all souls travel
thru
a traverse point in the cosmos protected
I live in all worlds exist in all things
place your palms to mine retrieve your memory

there's a TV screen in the third eye
viewing the Akashic record from the most high
trace your roots and return to the light
Hetapu.

## Mom Believed in Jesus

Mom believed in Jesus
but I'm a son of Obatala
evolution took me full circle
back to the beginning
before Black men hung from trees
whose roots grow deep as Ile Ife
emanating from the loins of Osun
not forced by slavers whips
into abandonment of ancestral visions
scars as deep as the Atlantic
middle passage in my DNA
memory everlasting
twisted and locked
liked Natty's dread
before the Romans
merged Heru and that dissident Apollonius of Tyanna
to invent the Lord of Lords that you call Jesus
before Europe's darkest age
when Elizabeth made twisted James the King
who hijacked Biblios Helios
and sold it to you as gospel
I came thru pyramids to kneel at obelisks
secrets of the Sphinx I sing
for man fears time but time fears the Sphinx
this Yidaki on my shoulders
sounded the world into being
I descended from the cosmos
sent by Oludumare on the web of spiders
before the Earth had seasons
you try to figure me out
not understanding the poetry nor the reason
you think I wear my hair this way
because of Rastafari
but these sacred antenna

are connections to the messengers of Gods
that existed long before him
so don't be fooled by photographs that only tell part of
the story
the soul has no beginning and no end
the kingdom of Heaven is within
and this is just an image of my holy temple.

# A Poet's Prayer to Obatala

Hepa Obatala
King of Creation
He who is owner of the White Cloth
owner of thoughts and dreams
Lord of Earth
I come to you in this time and place
I give homage for your blessings, your guidance, and your protection
the divination stated
that it is my destiny to channel your message
wrap me in your white cloth
protect me from my enemies
give me wisdom, calmness, and understanding
use my body, my mind, and my spirit
to speak peace and harmony into existence
in these days of turmoil and confusion
give me patience
anoint me with clarity as pure as your white cloth
to save humans from destruction
Oh Chief of the Sacred grove
Owner of Ori*
give me strength to light the darkness
He who creates at will
I bring to you
snail and pounded yam
shea butter and a white hen
I ask Esu to open the way
I ask Oya
let peace and justice come on the wind
I sing my song for you
Moforibale

Ase.

## Palm Sunday's Ritual

We go to Kings
pick up two pigeons
and two hens
carry them to Queens
curious subway onlookers
quietly ponder why there are
chickens but no dog or cat in the pet carrier crate
the lady in red
goes to receive Oya
but Shango demands a rooster
we pass by churches
parishioners carry palms
lately I find myself examining such contradictions
the gifts of Ifa and Obatala came to me at Christmas
the world is in such chaos
I seek relief from cowboy killture
from the land where my forefathers were stolen
returning to old time religions
following ancestors' visions
wondering what use is your God
with his hands and feet nailed to a cross?
Each morning in my shrine room
I prostrate and pray to Orishas
Babalawos read the secrets
the mat is spread for his Opele
Iyanifas read 256 Odus with 16 Cowries
Ma'at has 42 Laws
10 Commandments seem trite and insignificant
in comparison
so soon we forget there is but one God

no matter what you call it the Creator remains the same
there are many paths to the mountain top
time is unimportant to a tree
all things are connected
there is no life without water the evening blesses us with rain
in a world of war and contradictions
We leave ebo at the crossroads
and pray for peace.

## Eleri Ipin*

Ifa is the witness of destiny
the authority in this divinity
so when one door was shut
a new one opened
she came saying
she was Osun's Daughter
with an aura so compelling
I knew we'd be together at first sight
now I know that sounds presumptuous
but I was truly enraptured by her charm
and the jazz of her beauty
captured my attention
like the lure of a new dimension
I guess one would think I'd be cautious
trying to woo this river goddess
taking me to places not explored
at least not by me
like leaving offerings by a tree
for mothers
on a snowy midnight
but remember
Ifa is the witness of destiny
the authority in this divinity
when one door shuts
another will open
as I was guided to the Babalawo
on a path that I had long been seeking
Esu opened the way
it was on the day of my solar return
that I learned I would be crowned Obatala
and that metamorphosis would come
in the winter of my life
on the backs of my ancestors' visions
so remember Ifa is the witness of destiny

the authority in this divinity
when one door shuts
another will open
as I left offerings at the crossroad
at midnight
that opened the way to my journey
to Ibadan
tin roofs and roosters crowing
awakening to a new day dawning
a rebirth to give praise to Oludumare
for long life, good health, and prosperity
Moforibale

Ase.

# Countdown to 65 - Poem 13

I've been digging thru the contradictions
trying to find my way back to beginnings
walking in circles spiral
searching for the light
I've been turning over rocks
studying how his-story turns back clocks
redefining definitions,
separating spirit from apparition,
searching catacombs and caves
found out secrets that were amazing
deciphered my way thru mazes
trying to find the way,
studied Bibles, Mctu Neter,
the Tao, the Koran and texts from mystery schools
philosophers, scholars, and fools
searched books to find Jesus
found that he was no Christian
now I question his existence
and understand your resistance
to believe these things I'm finding
but I question that book you call the Bible
wondering who we should hold liable
for the survival of these lies
distorted scriptures in disguise.
Heru was the Sun God,
misinterpreted as God's son
make sure to look closely you can see
Ausar, Auset, and Heru:
the Holy Trinity.
As written in the Book of Coming Forth by Day
Greeks call it Biblios Helios
it's real name is the Sun Book
these doctrines need investigation
since the Nicaean convention

when rulers changed the holy text
so you won't know what's coming next
full deception to control by fear
got you believing in revelations
ignoring reincarnation
thinking that the end is near
so be conscious of what you read
these rulers lie and deceive
then perhaps you'll make the decision
to return to your ancestors' vision.

# Whose Civilization?

Epigraph:

"beware false prophets
who come with offering plates
religion is free" ~ Ngoma

Religious persecution
is deadly
like the Spanish Inquisition
forced on your consciousness
at the point of a saber
now crucifixes hanging from the barrel of machine guns
got me pondering the definition
of civilization
in gold we trust
all else is suspect
burned at the stake
declared as fake
whiplashed til you cry "Toby!"
desecrated by God's soldiers
third eyes circumcised
blindly following the blind
forever lost in darkness
searching for the light
whose civilization is it anyway
coerced into thinking
your God's better than mine
ancient mysteries stolen
land traded for Bibles
scarification denials
looking in mirrors
seeking to recover
true identity.

## They Walk Thru Life with Eyes Wide Shut

In denial that their tv sets lied,
that their holy books are plagiarized
by amnesia patients
suffering post-traumatic stress
since the Spanish Inquisition
trading land for beads and Bibles
to those who could not read
then forced to believe
that the cross would save them
they said believe us
but it didn't save Jesus
Immaculate Conception
reincarnation
resurrection
or suffer the wrath of the sword
in those days of dark called medieval
ruled by societies' secrets
degrees and planets
evicted from temples
numbers keepers
King James, the filthy, drunken pervert
seized the scrolls
and flipped the scripture
but never got instructions
to decipher the inscriptions
passed down by master teachers
otherwise known as Egyptians
so tell me
who's defining this definition
did he fit the description
in the lineup of those accused of treason
tell me Buddha
what do you think

of this new guy Jesus
should we ask Krishna
if he's come to confuse us
after all crusaders
burn witches at the stake
so was he sent to deceive us
with the veil of misconception
that there was only one
Immaculate Conception
crucifixion
resurrection
well first you'd better take a look
at the planets ancient mystery books
it doesn't take a CSI
to know there were thieves in the temple.
Word! That lying Judas
you mean he didn't speak of
Horus or Attis,
Khrishna or Dionysus,
Buddha or Mithra
and those of every family
you'd best to find the righteous path
learn the science and the math
to play the dozens
to every thing there is a season
12 tribes = 12 disciples = 12 constellations
or planets around Horus the Sun
the secret of life is one.
How do I know this you ask?
At high noon I shape shifted into a dove
I was there
when he stood
in a circle squared.

## Morning Meditations

Each morning
I go to my shrine room to pray
for Elegba to open the way
Osala anoints me with clarity
optimism eludes me
reality stands in the way
so I leave offerings at the cross road
riding on a cloud of cigar smoke
I bring rum and machetes to the party
Obatala wraps his white cloth around me
from my enemy I am protected
the divination ordained me
to speak truth to power
Shango brings the fire
Ogun's got my back with his shield of iron
my lantern is lit
to bring darkness to light
spiritually connected
the Egun guide me
they speak to me
so I translate
they say we must continue to fight the good fight
the victory is certain
but we must unite
they say not to fear
that time is on our side
we must pay close attention
to the winds of change
all impurities from the earth will be purged
only then will the voice of the oppressed be heard
stand firm listen to the Oracle
remember in the beginning
there was the word.

## Sitting on the Edge of Tomorrow

So I'm sitting on the edge of tomorrow
making ebo to Obatala.
He says peace and justice is coming
patience is the father of good character
I hear war drums in the distance
but I ain't sweatin'
me and Ogun been tight since 'Nam
so I spray him with some gin
give him some palm oil,
a Black Pig and the head of a dog
'Legba telling me
"There's always at least two sides to this thing:
choose the red pill or the blue pill"
there's a rumble between the Eagle and the Bear
but the Dragon's sitting on the sideline
waiting for the empire to fall
all the news is fake
while the sheeple pray to false Messiahs
but Ifa says
"Victory is destined to the righteous
and the Army of Light
will prevail over darkness!"

Ase.

## Residue on the Altar of Time

Time has such short memory
as things evolve into other things
like ice into water
steam to rain
puddles to oceans
it's all the same
depending how you look at it
or which way it looks at you
20/20 vision to the woke
Lady Liberty blindfolded
world turned upside down
no longer a metaphor
visions of impeaching the whole cabinet
rise to the top
like stench from the shitstem in decay
so we close the door on a decade
don't let optimism escape you
depression is a hard row to hoe
ancestors humming
we didn't come this far not to make it
don't be dismayed as things go in circles
there'll be a phoenix in the ashes
remember
energy has no beginning
and no end
change is eternal
fear is wasted
for time is an illusion
like residue in the altar of your memory
what mark will you leave on eternity?

# *Music Is my Essence*

## I'm a String Scientist

Don't mean to brag
but I'ma string scientist
my first axe was an umbilical cord
next a vocal cord
you might say
it had that good vibration
by kindergarten
I was thumpin' phat bass lines
on a rubber band
next I figured out the answers
to the riddle of the fiddle
and how to make a string sing
soon I learned to make a piano
do what it do
I looked inside and realized
it had strings too
the cello was next in line
between my knees I stroked it
til it sounded fine
freedom songs and the guitar
became friends of mine
intoxicated with jazz I played an upright bass
I was one of the first to put
funk in your face
love of the blues brought an African Banjo
my finger dexterity is supreme you see
now I'm looking for the next string gizmo
uh, I'm not your average string thing
I'm a string scientist.

## A Love Story

it was at a Sunday evening church program that we first met
I'd also seen her once or twice at school
it was a kindergarten crush turned into a love affair
we'd often walk to school together
who would have thought it may last forever
it was really love at first sight
and once I heard her sing
I knew there was no turning back
she was a smooth brown with perfect curves
and once I got up the nerve to touch her perfect body
it resulted in a sweet vibrato
sometimes she'd come to my music practice room
it was just large enough for a piano
up on the third floor
we'd close the door for a minuet or two
it was my finger dexterity
and sensuous stroke that made the music float
like foreplay licking your ear
one day she says to me "Look this vanilla sex is bland
and if you want me to stay, you'd best to find a plan
cause a sister like me wants to be heard"
so 'bout that time I got her amped
she liked the way I played her pedals
when I plugged her in we went to another level
as the music soared it was electric
we both loved phat bass lines with funk in the trunk
you might say I had her in the pocket
when we rocked it the earth resonated
when my fingertips plucked string
you could hear her sing like a band of gypsies
on a summer nite
she was a sweet thing

never jealous when I fingered the flute
or sweetly kissed the didgeridoo
it was a menage a trois of sweet harmony
that's why my first love was my violin.

## A Poem in Response to the Question What Kind of Music Do You Play?

Swallow sweet sound like Quinine
dog faced blues
music junkies
acquired taste for flatted fifths
reggae skankin' bubblin' bass
funk in yo face
ghost of Hendrix
defiant strings
ragga muffin style
heartbeat Nyabinghi
diaspora sound for the melanin enhanced
jungle dance on concrete
unboxable improvisational freestyle buck wild
music notation can't chart this
culture bandits can't steal this
it's too real for Memorex
we string scientist
do voodoo mathematics on your ear hole
funk so deep
Grammys can't judge stolen blues
from Mali to Memphis
cipher spinning on and on
from bebop to hip hop
eternity's too short for this rhyme in future time
only the righteous can sing this song.

## Fiddle Me This

It's a string thing
you wouldn't understand
but since I was seven
I've had this fiddle in my hands
doing my thing with strings
my violin has women jealous
cause of my finger dexterity
these licks run up your spine
while you try to figure out
how to box this
from Bach to jazz fusion, it's unboxable
I rock this funky assed sound from underground
careful, your neck could snap
trying to make your head
nod to this
these strokes make love to your
ear hole
making the connections
from your chakras to your soul
Afrika embedded in my DNA
if you listen you can tell from the roots I play
deeper than a million diamond mines
you'll hear her screaming over funky bass lines
like a noisy lover
experiencing a first time multiple eargasm
I'm the fiddler in the hood
I'm the answer to the ancient riddle
tell me - who's Dr Rock-a-Fiddle?

## String (In Memory of Billie Bang)

You gotta learn the math
to understand the science
like how many vibrations it takes
to hit the crown chakra
it's in the scream of the string
the glissando it sings
how to make the bottom root
and hold on
climb up your spine
explode in your ears
definition unreachable
gotta be able to play in
to understand where out is
so you can find the way home
more than knowing the fingering
up on the down stroke
to bring an eargasm
pluck harmonic double stops
and chromatic overtones
like kora sounds
multiplicity surrounds
sweat 'til your dues are paid
release your demons
no short cuts to this song of evolution
there is no open door
'til your ears mature
it can take lifetimes
until your sound is found
channeling ancestral visions
at the crossroads.

## Brown Butterfly

Seven is one
trickster
and triple threat
non-believer of impossible
he who threw the stone today
that killed the chicken yesterday
ancestral conversations
channeling warrior spirit
impossible
absent from lexicon
no Plan B
only the inevitability of victory
only the victory of destiny
deliverer of prayers to heaven
telepathic decisions
the right path
at the crossroads
in four directions
like a weathervane  summoning Oya
synergy of speed and rhythm
synergy of thought and action
synergy of wit and tongue
inside and outside are only illusions
victory is only the other side of conquest
triumph comes from refusing defeat
conquering is the decision made before battle
agreements made
before entering the marketplace of life
service is the rent one pays
for space on the planet
only true believers
evolve in this equation
existence always
hangs in the balance of destiny

destiny always hangs in the balance
of existence
fists of iron
forged on anvils
deep in the forest
sharpening of cutlass
cunning is necessary
in a dog-eat-dog existence
hunters, farmers even Kings
we come bearing
head of a dog
covered in gin and red palm oil
hot pepper stew
Ebo made to Ogun
Ijala drum rhythms
beat of the cosmos
blood and fire
blood, blood, and fire
when blood comes out
to gaze at the sky
Oya fans the flames
war dance and mind games
jungle dance on concrete
thought is faster than light
telepathy faster than sound
on the path to triumph
deals made with the blacksmith
sharpening fists like machetes
to cut away injustice
blinding like sand in a whirlwind
burying imbalances
upon your sword
a piece of iron
a measure of earth
no one dare swear falsely
frequency electric

swiftness beyond measure
riding on the wind
truth the great destroyer
the needle is sharp on both ends
protector of the oppressed
champion of the downtrodden
oh, son of Ogun
lay down your cutlass
and hunt no more
darer and conqueror of traditions
Black Centipede
Oh, son of Ogun
Muhammad Ali
master of the forge, father of Ijala poets
I write this poem for you
may it mark your place
amongst the ancestors
we see you in the wind
when Oya blows
and the road is still famished.

# We String Scientists

A 440's vibrations
just a measure of sound to we
string scientists who be bending thangs between the keys
you be wondering how we make strings scream
our fingaz interpret transcendental dreams
you wonder why we don't play Bach
we say these strings were born to rock
we amped and sing electric sound
octaves divided and roots in the ground
we define this sound we sing walking up your spine
with the funk we bring
we like phat bass lines and hot grooves
to be like life - we like to keep it smooth
maybe with a slice of p-funk on the side
my fiddle got a mind of her own
one day told me she wanted to be a saxophone
she's gangster breaks all the europe-peons
so-called classical laws
says I don't play that dead white folks shit
bitch-jazz rules
we serve a full menu from bebop to hip hop
with a side order of field holla blues
from my Afrikan muse
we past, present, and future tense
elevating minds with resonance
bringing vibrational healing
call it chakras or sacroiliac
from root to crown
just inhale this music down
like a puff puff pass let the sound go deep
then close your eyes exhale repeat
peace love and spiritual prosperity
peace love and spiritual prosperity
peace love and spiritual prosperity.

## D.W.B. (Didj'n While Black) - A True Story from the Village of Harlem

Epigraph: I'm a musician that plays an array of instruments. One of them is the Yidaki, an Australian Aboriginal drone instrument otherwise known as a didjeridoo (didj for short). It's a tubular instrument about 4 1/2 ft long which I carry in a mud cloth bag with a strap on my shoulder. It's an Om sounding instrument often used for meditation. Its sound creates a trance state called the dreamtime.

So I'm strollin' thru Harlem bout midnite
on the way home from a poetry spot
didj on my shoulder as usual
just chillin' being casual
cause I'm cool like that
but you probably already know that
by the way I wear my hat
it's an ole school thang
I'm sure you understand
it's part of fitting the description
of a Black man.
Anyway, I digress although I'm pretty cool
I need to get this off my chest
I just don't need the stressin'
but these stupid cops be messin' with a brother
like I'm carrying a bazooka in my bag
or some weapon of mass destruction or something.
Anyway, they come up cruisin' real slow
checking me out like they was in doubt
whether to call back up from Homeland Security
like I was a terrorist and they should be scared of me
radio cracklin' in the background
I get a chill in my spine as I turn around
wondering why the hell they be following me

remembering their stop and frisk policy.
They pull up to the curb
get out of the squad car saying "Excuse me, sir,
we'd like to know what you're carrying in your bag?"
I started to get an attitude
but it was two young Black overseers
so I decided not to sound rude
cause I didn't want to end up like Diallo.
Pulling it slowly out of my bag
as I said
"Y'all relax, it's a musical instrument,
just give me a moment and I'll demonstrate."
creating the hypnotic sound
didn't want to be spread eagle on the ground
now I'm wondering if Harlem's gentrification
had anything to do with creating this ill situation
and if there would have been
a violation of my rights
If my skin was white?

## This Bloody Business Called Music
## (for Etta James, Don Cornelius, Whitney Houston, and Michael Jackson)

Epigraph - You may not want to call it a conspiracy, but in my humble opinion, when famous artists' net worth becomes more when they're dead than when they're alive, their untimely death becomes very suspicious

If you look real good
on a full moon night
they tell me you can see the buzzards
circling hollyweird when the spotlights go out
that's why it's called show business
but there's no show without the cash flow
so you're only as good as
the platinum sale of your latest record
and the pressure starts
long before the disc drops
on your mark, get set - BANG
and the race is on
to see if profit beats expenses
to the finish line
nobody gives a damn that it's all an illusion
that you're stacking cash
while drowning in debt
partying hard to wash away the pain
of living a lie
everyone wants to be the judge
as the papparazzi collects photos where the exposure
shows you're only human
the tabloids print lies about
your life placed on the auction block
using the images like slaves

assassinating character
a case without a trial
or like Tupac, you only have a record
now that you have a record deal
and more money to escape
with drugs and booze
and sex and pills
and flashy cars and big mansions
that took the place of family
each night when the curtains closed
there's a new town with a mint on your pillow
a new chauffeur, a new limo,
a new stage, and another spotlight waiting
producers, hangers-on, and bill collectors shape
shift into vampires
sucking creative blood from veins
welcome to the dark side
with everyone begging for a ride
on your merry go round
life becomes a circus
but the credit cards maxed out
nobody told you
that the royalties are done
you don't own the rights to the songs
too high to read the small print in the contract
as everyone wants to be the judge and the jury
of how a well-paid doctor and a hand full of pills
were the answer to the question
that nobody took the time to ask
meanwhile the producer counts the cash
before they pull your dead drenched carcass
from the pool
the beat goes on
ka ching.

## Jazz Doesn't Live Here Anymore

Me and Mz Queen stepped off the train
125th and Lenox
dressed to the nines feeling fine
hyped 'bout being in Harlem
cause it's the mecca
the place to give homage
the space that birthed
Duke's "Take the A Train"
we real cool
planning on checking out the scene
looking for the hotspots like the Baby Grand
but there's a closed sign on the door
and we notice the ghost
of all the hot spots that have disappeared
so here we stand on sacred ground:
The Cotton Club,
"Just Be Simple's" birthplace
across 110th to 155$^{th}$ river to river
home of the Lindy Hop
and the Audubon where Malcolm was shot,
place where Marcus Garvey
recruited for the Black Star Line
home of the cool where the women are fine
the place Sammy hoofed
and Ben E King sang "Stand By Me,"
where they listened to Coleman Hawkins
danced to Tito Puente in El Barrio
watched hip hop poets in a cypher
puff puff passing rhymes
danced the Harlem Shuffle decades before the
Harlem Shake
watched Bojangles and Sandman, too,
James Brown at the Apollo
before Michael Jackson was a thoughtform

from the Lindy Hop to bebop to hip hop
now all of the legacy
has been closed, sold out, and bought
not even the Red Rooster crows like it used to
where Adam Clayton Powell ate breakfast
before Sunday's service at Abyssinia
so it's got me wondering
how can this legacy be saved
or will it be like a cemetery
with a tombstone that says
JAZZ DOESN'T LIVE HERE ANYMORE.

## Music Is My Essence

It started with the rhythm of the down stroke
the yin and yang of love
creation of heartbeat in the womb
first smack on the bottom
the dissonant melody of my first note
the song of my cry
gospel music harmony was my ear training
bass line tattooed on my umbilical cord
wiggling my toes to the back beat
music lessons on my mother's knee
she was the Sunday school pianist
seven was the magic number
captured by the riddle of the fiddle
it was my first-string thing
music notation became a second language
in sixth grade a flute joined the family
followed by a keyboard and a cello
high school brought
my baritone horn to the marching band
Civil Rights sit-ins and anti-war love-ins
birthed the age of folk music but freedom songs
brought me a guitar
mentored by Odetta (whom I later met)
and Nina vicariously Bob Dylan and John Lennon
in rotation on my turntable
doo wop on the corner and basement quarter parties
jazz came late at night caressing my ear drums
In defiance of my size
finally large enough to rock an upright bass
riding the A Train to a "Night in Tunisia"
then came Serious Bizness/Serious Music
for serious times: just two voices and a guitar
from Central Park to Madison Square Garden,
London, Germany, and Paris

our songs embraced the earth
kissed by new age music
surrendered to the Yidaki's healing sound
didgeridoo is a misnomer like jigaboo
African rhythms took me on the journey,
congas, shekere, mini bata drum
Mali to Memphis, Benin to Brooklyn,
deep South Afrikan banjo strum
my music teacher told me
it's the music that keeps us young
music is my essence.

## *All the Blues That's Fit to Read*

## Why Newspapers Are Becoming Obsolete

Democracy begs for change on the subway
stuck underground like a rat in the tunnel
never to see the sunshine of truth
lost in a maze of abbreviated newspapers
paid for by advertisers only giving you news
on sales of overpriced merchandise
marked down to keep your attention
from reality
after all, if the truth be known
there'd be riots in the street
not the kind instigated by the CIA in the Middle East
but a struggle for existence
in the yet to be United States of Amerikkka
owned by China, mortgaged by Britain, run by Israel,
managed by Rothschild
truth hidden so deep
it can't see the light of the sun, son,
economy feeling like a merry go round
going up and down
the Dow Jones average
spinning round and round
oil gushing out of the ground
so Google imperalism
oxymoronic humanitarian war is inhumane
we still being tricked by the same old game
but war fills the coffins
so things remain the same
just repeating the past
but begging for change.

## Who Killed Orphan Annie?

There are those who think
gays are being persecuted
for defying divine order
but if God made everything
does he make mistakes?
What would Jesus say
when abortion centers are bombed?
Would he ask if doctors' lives
were less valuable
than fetuses?
Then what of endless wars?
Is it written in your Holy Babble
that your sons give up their lives
for opium and oil?
Is the world turned upside down?
How will you tell your daughters
that the fruit of their wombs
may never see the sunrise
sentenced to death by old men
with lost souls
who send children off to fight their battles
and take food from the mouths of babes
to pay for megaton bombs
that destroy the homes, jobs, and hospitals
of the newly dispossessed
who now wander the earth like a walkabout,
searching for a way to rebuild
the puzzle of their existence
flinging stones at goliath
pledging to the republic
masquerading as a democracy
pleading with Daddy Warbucks
to wash his bloody hands
blind to the fact
Orphan Annie is dead?

## My Pen's Got a Point

It's a gloomy day in gotham
even the sky weeps
two trips around the sun short of half a century
since the King of love was killed
Malcolm's cry for self determination
short circuited by civil rights still absent
the debt of reparations still not paid
peckerwoods disillusioned
Confederate battle rags taped to their consciousness
brains on lockdown
illiterate believers in the Holy Babble
wishing for the good ole days
when strange fruit hung from poplar trees
ghost of Hitler reincarnated
Klansmen dressed in suits of blue
water hoses replaced by teargas
tanks and FEMA camps on standby
for the coming Armageddon
gentrification is ethnic cleansing
land of the free
home of the brave
doomsday looms on the horizon
as we pray this is a nightmare
I'm afraid my tongue was handcuffed
struggling to sound the alarm
hoping you read this poem of liberation
before the Fifth Amendment is taken hostage
and thinking is outlawed
I'm just glad my pen's got a point.

## B4 the End of the World

If you think I'm sexy
let me know
cause we could get it on before
these mad men blow up the world
I could be your bridge
from the past to the future
cause the future
doesn't present much hope
and I'm looking for an alternative to war
maybe a dark beer and
a Natty Dread woman
who practices ganja inhalation meditation
I want to taste the THC on her tongue
take me to some other place
deep between her thighs
I want to contemplate her navel from the inside
search for answers to questions like
what makes her juices flow?
And I'm looking for an end to rhetoric
there's a battle going on to capture your mind
surround yourself in light
forget your prayers
instead of trying to talk to God
meditate
God will talk to you
listen to the silence
it's maybe the only good news available
as lost souls cry out the truth
sacrifices to injustice
victims of the world's disorder
beware of bushes that burn
wake up and piss
the world's on fire
I saw it on the news the other day

some mad men with stolen passports
men of no property
who love death more than women
and freedom more than anything
set fire to Twin Towers and the Pentagon
snake eyes came up like skeletons
the stench of rotting corpses poisons Wall Street
wrapped in Ole Gory
the Dow tumbles like a drunk
down a dark stairwell
an amnesia victim
forgetting all the crimes she has committed
pleading not guilty
in a court of insanity
a cacophony of stolen elections
genocidal reflections
and wars that rage on since Solomon's temples
so choose the red pill or the blue pill if you will
you who scoffed when told to behold
that the horse was pale
liberty is stuck at the airport
bags being searched by the National Guard
cheeks spread, raped again
like Hiroshima, Nagasaki, Vietnam, Grenada, and Haiti
the news is controlled by Disney
the fantasy on your TV is stark reality
only you have the power to change it
put down your flag
it cannot protect you from the karma.

## I Don't Believe God Did This

I need poles
I can fish for my damn self
y'all my God's better than your God motherfuckers
really piss me off
besides God don't do earthquakes
some dude in Canada got the contract
he was a union buster
disaster is profitable
and just like New Orleans
you'd better bet Haitians
won't get the job building barracks for U.S. military
occupation
cause Phat Sam looks for ways to fatten his war chest
besides he needs more cheap labor to manufacture
the bullshit your TV says you need to get by
so please send some water, some food, and some
aspirin
we've got a hell of a headache
but please keep your soldiers
we got no time for war
your security always created coups
with small print on the bullets
and governments that fall like dominoes
changing presidents faster than changing drawers
with those high interest IMF loans
International Money Fuckers
so don't lecture me about profanity
there's nothing more profane than poverty
I think Ogun on the war path leveled Catholic
churches
and I've seen the devil
he looks like Pat Robertson
and Haitians didn't make a pact with him
the tourist boats still land 25 miles from Port au Prince

and the Dominican Republic
but the poor still can't get medicine nor food to eat
and after Pearl Harbor, Oklahoma, 9/11, Katrina
Iraq, Afghanistan, and FEMA
I'm just not convinced God did this.

## His Story

There are more ghosts here than in old boneyards
sufferers of the hangman's noose
or burned at the stake
before New York was a city
when Wall Street really had a wall
that separated slaves
from the savages that brought them in chains
to a growing metropolis
where no one thinks of slavery anymore
there are more ghosts here than in old boneyards
you can hear them in the wind
blowing from the Hudson where once there were docks
that unloaded them like cargo
naked and freezing in the winter rain
there are more ghosts here than in old boneyards
footprints left on cobblestones
barefoot in the snow
before being auctioned off like cattle
wheat, molasses, and tobacco
woven dry goods from Morocco
there are more ghosts here than in old boneyards
Africans and indentured white men
accused of conspiring to fight for freedom
branded as witches
hanged in chains to decompose
some banished and transported
no historical markers to be noted
tales left out of His Story books
stories that may never be told
yes, my friends

there are more ghosts here than in old boneyards
ancestral spirits rise from the ashes
as the phoenix of Weeksville reincarnates
telling stories of free Black men
who built homes, schools, churches,
banks, and burial grounds
yes, there are more ghosts here than ole boneyards
if you listen to Oya at midnight.
You might hear Biggie singing
"Spread love-It's the Brooklyn way"

## Funktastic

If I were meant to be controlled
I would have come with a remote
but funk is eternal
so I'm real careful where I stick my finger
cause I know bullshit when I smell it
and if these elections were effective
they'd be illegal
I'm praying that my folk
go out and feel the Bern
it's the only way to expose the truth
but if I was a betting man
I'd put my money on corruption
cause these motherfuckers
tryin ta start sumpn'
and soups coming to a boil
I aint feeling the flava
so I'm playing two sides against the middle
using my Mastercard
charging tickets on the Black Star Line
just in case things get foul
cause word is out
that even the Pope is building an army
Armageddon might be more
than gibberish in the Holy Babble
and I got 'Legba on speed dial
my advice to you is that we gotta unite
to shift this paradigm
i got 7 Babalawos on stand-by
I'm on that mothership
meanwhile
I hope y'all been doing your third eye lid lifts.

# Java

Dear Starbucks,
the line in my poem
"Tryin ta Pay off Student Loans
with Salaries from Starbucks"
was in no way intended to offend you.
The real question we ask is
why the U.S. economy can't provide
adequate employment for me to be able to repay
the loans on my three degrees with minimum wage
and in this so-called land of plenty
home of the American Dream where nothing is as it seems?
Why can't education be free?
Actually Starbucks
we thank you for giving us the opportunity
to be employed
in this land of the free
where so many have lost their jobs
so we work for you
unorganized and non-union
it's the American Dream turned nightmare
homogenized and deculturized
ignoring the pleas of our third world kin
as child labor picks your beans
while half the world
is strung out on sugar and caffeine
lined up to get your overpriced fix
to start the day
like crack fiends
I must admit your product is supreme
got folks dreaming
the American Dream.

## Starfuck

It only took two minutes
the barista figured
colored folk should only be
picking coffee
not drinking it
maybe waiting on folk
not waiting for folk
the overseers asked no questions
still mad that Assata was free
and Mumia still alive
common sense was not on the menu
they were still hired
after failing sensitivity training
not feeling that the niggas
had rights to be read before being arrested
after all this was Illadelphia
the City of Otherly Love
or love for white folk only
where those of darker hue
are tolerated as long as they
stay in their lane.
Emancipation Proclamation
hadn't been taught in school
I guess miseducation said that we were
happy slaves
the kneegrow chief of overseers
claimed no apology was needed
after all he was blue first
when the #BoycottStarbucks signs arrived
the plantation boss realized
that the cash flow was
about to be interrupted
damage control could save his bottom line
while saving his behind

he's praying that with racial sensitivity training
might redeem him
but sadly not much has changed
in this four-hundred-year conversation.

## Convo with Rod

Uh huh
y'all be be callin' me lotsa names:
Roscoe, Rod, Equalizer, God,
Magnum, Peashooter, Hardware, Blaster,
aka gun
seems I'm known for fortune, fun, and fame
but recently I'm the one taking all the blame
problem is y'all be actin' buck wild
indicting me without a trial
it's like some kind of conspiracy
to always be blaming me
without the bullet and finger that pulls the trigger
yeah, you heard that right, guns don't shoot people
without the people who shoot guns
it's that hypocrisy from y'all spouters
of the Good Book that says "Thou shalt not kill"
now, I know I may be sounding rude
but some a y'all got bad attitudes
thinking you're supreme and starting fights
shooting everything in sight
just because your skin is white
aw now, don't get your panties all in a bunch
thinking I'm out to lunch
cause I ain't trying to hear it
so, if the glove don't fit, don't wear it
but instead of gun control
how about control your gun?
I think it's time to change your murderous mentality,
rid yourself of that colonizer state of mind
thinking entitlement of all you find
how about eradicating fear
acting like Armageddon is here?
There's enough to go around
for all to share

now could be a time for peace
everything could actually be fine
til then when you put down yours
I'll put down mine.

## Bloodstained Handprints on the Wailing Wall (For Palestine)

The empire has new clothes
but the strings are pulled
by the same puppeteer
the general's closet is opened wide
skeletons tumbling like dominoes
gossip on every channel
quite a distraction from important things
but you know that little thing inside your head
that keeps you from saying things you shouldn't ...
I don't have one of those
my wingman's on vacation
I'm staring truth in the face
realizing that the east has no middle
and there's no peace on the Mount of Olives
with Uranus squaring Pluto
artillery shells lobbed back and forth
like Wimbledon without a referee
hear no evil, see no evil, speak no evil
gives us some illusions
that there is no karma
if all the killing is done by drones
the trigger has no soul
history books burned
the rent is late on leased memories
everyone running for the border
no one knowing where it is
yet claiming they were there first
drawing lines in the sands of time
altered by windstorms
schizophrenic escapees from holocaust ovens
confuse sovereignty with terrorism
the death count grows steadily
integrity takes a vacation

legs spread like a general's side piece
bloodstained handprints on the wailing wall.

## Opinion of a Fly on the Wall (Trick or Treat)

If you see me flying around
you know there's some foul shit somewhere
that's why I landed on the VP's head
on nationwide TV
just like we told you before
so much shit's going on
that there's a shortage of toilet paper
shit like T-Rump faking the coronavirus
next week he'll be selling stock in the cure
meanwhile
thousands die
while he lies
now he tells us
mouthwash cures COVID
like the universe is constipated
and needs a laxative
cause there's a back up
in this cesspool
as the selection election lie
spreads faster than a California wildfire
and the NFA crew
is armed to the teeth
cause we are our ancestors' wildest dream
masked and speaking in tongues
you think it's gibberish
but we are but
a microcosm of a macrocosm
a reflection of the everything
and Big-Eyed Jimmy told you
there would be Fire Next Time
but why believe me
I'm just a fly on the wall.

## Sneakaz

Hate to break it down to you this way
but no
basketball is not revolution
and we need to end all confusion
and disillusion and find a solution
while Cise and Cedisa earn
one dollar 85 cents a day
as you play
less than the cost of a Nike shoelace
forced labor in your face
dunk this swish, swish
give me a star on which to wish
wish away this poverty
exploitation is all I see
eleven dollars and ten cents a week as we speak
just trying to keep your family fed
might earn you a sneaker upside your head
if you're slow
Nike trips up on workers' rights
twelve-hour days with only five hours sleep at night
meanwhile here under the stars and bars
Nike's ceo named Knight
bankroll higher than a kite
porfolio eight point five billion
yachts and planes and company trillions
still a pair of Nikes cost three month's salary
for worker's begging on their knees in Vietnamese
yeah, I hear you wondering
what the hell's that got to do with me and you
chillin- watchin' the tube under the blood splattered
banner red, white, and blue?
Well, Michael Jordan earns 40 million dollars a year
just to let Nike use his name
twice as much as shootin' hoops

which incidentally was his only claim to fame
quietly playing ball cause he's got no balls
but Nike pays brothas well
not to show and tell
besides he's busy space jammin with Bugs Bunny
playing golf making all that money
meanwhile Spike, he's gotta have it,
a 40 thousand dollar pair of seasons tickets to the Knicks
plus a few million duckets for commercials
so much for rehearsals
hey Spike take a leaflet
read about the worker's plight
I ain't got time, I'm trying to get a taxi for my wife
while a 12-year-old takes a nine to the dome
murdered for his sneakers while trying to get home
one more brother laid to rest
a bullet in his head and chest
another brother candidate for the penitentiary gate
creating jobs for redneck prison guards in the joint
you get my point
so you can register and vote as fast as you can
but the robber barons laid a master plan
candidates call them on the phone
grand boule and skull and bone
those with 33 degrees
keeping people on their knees
with old world money and new world disorder
they think they can do anything they please
watch out for these secret societies
Sneakaz-Just Do It

## The State of Emergency That Nobody Told You About or the Low Down on the Down Low (Conspiracy Theory 101)

Epigraph:

Hold your fire, don't shoot the messenger
though I know that this message be stressin' ya
I'm a mirror, I just reflect what I see
please don't shoot me I'm not the enemy.

Listen carefully and pay attention
this poem will not be on Facebook,
will not be on Youtube or Twitter,
will not be published in an anthology,
and will not be on the five o'clock news.
This poem will self-destruct upon completion
just like free jazz improvisation
it will never be experienced again.
This poem is to tell you
that all the news is fake
owned by the same motherfuckers
that don't want you to know
that they are motherfuckers
Democrats and Republicans
are just opposite sides of the same coin
they hang out and have drinks
snort coke and fuck the same underage
boys and girls from the secret pedophile ring
in the White House at the end of the workday
truth be told
they don't run anything anyway
it's just a facade
there is no government
it all belongs to the Federal Reserve

run by the Bilderbergs, the Masons, the Skull and Bones,
the Illuminati, the Jesuits, and Secret Societies
your birth certificate and social security number
are a bank note payable in blood when you die
but nobody told you
it's all in the books:
Behold a Pale Horse, The Occult Conspiracy,
and the Truth Shall Set You Free by David Eick
you can still find them overpriced on Amazon
copies are limited or may be out of print
Steve Cokely exposed it years ago on Youtube
the Holy Bible is fiction designed to control you
actually, it's an astrology book
you think I'm talking heresy
if Jesus really saves
he would have done it already
but he couldn't save himself
I turned off the president's speech
it's all an illusion anyway
social media is a government experimental
mind control mechanism on your computer
and your mobile device
everything you do is being watched
and recorded by your TV
immigration detention camps
are rehearsals for martial law
global warming is controlled by HAARP
no, HAARP is not a musical instrument
it's not the mayor of Elm City either
I don't have time to explain it
but it's not too late to Google it
the Housing Projects are part of the Rockefeller plan
It was a Yale Experiment, so is gentrification
the food at McDeath Burgers, Kentucky Died and ISlop

is fake too, designed to prepare you for Soylent Green
the new world disorder is sitting on your doorstep
when the doorbell rings don't answer
if you act now, it's not too late to stop it
Trumpleskinthin is a fake president
Mumia told me resistance works
but justice still rides in the back of the bus
so where's John Brown when you need him
remember struggle will set you free
don't forget you never heard any of this from me
this poem is a last warning
it will now self-destruct
five, four, three, two, one…

Poof.

## Pick Up Whatever You Can Pick up

A real education is important
ignorance is expensive
otherwise
one could go thru life
too dumb to know you're dumb,
too stupid to know you're stupid,
and too racist to know you're racist
it may even cause
the selection of a presididn't
who can't tell the bad guys from the bad guys
it's a real problem
if you watch a FOX Channel
not realizing it's the fox guarding the hen house
thinking CNN, the FBI, and CIA intelligence
are fake news
you can't put the genie back into the bottle
or make the president presidential
while the world's being turned upside down
leaving global warming deniers in charge
and we're stuck
at trying to figure out
if the so-called Constitution is constitutional?
Actually, everybody is an immigrant
except victims of the transatlantic slave trade
and indigenous first nation people
the real homeland security
should take back Mexico, Texas, California,
and Florida, too,
in fact maybe everybody should be deported
whose descendants came in boats
Mexicans should put up a wall to keep Cheeto out
you do realize that war is profitable
but the US hasn't won one
since 1945

seems like the new Confederacy is south of Canada
Trumpleskinthin
and the see no evil, hear no evil, speak no evil
cabinet
turns a blind eye to
hurricanes in Puerto Rico, California burning,
mud slides, massive oil leaks,
and the North Pole meltdown
seems like deja vu
20,000 years in a cave
can do strange things to a person's mind
so these so-called white supremacist
are under some kind of illusion
that they are supreme
and neo-slavery can make Amerikkka great again
seems to me it's time to
wake up from this nightmare
called the American Dream
cause these misleaders
change the rules of the game
faster than they change drawers
while you don't even realize
that it is a game
but there can be no peace without justice
and we keep forgetting to forget
that justice and laws
are two different conversations
so look here Lucy
we got a problem
while we're discussing sexual misconduct
the shit hole in the oval office is
sodomizing the whole damn world
without grease or a kiss
the Kremlin's got remote control
of the White House
as they try to make you think taking a knee

was about the anthem and the blood splattered banner
meanwhile Blue Lives still murder
while Black Lives Matter
sickos want to make you think
that pedophilia is normal
and should be legal
but there's a secret pedophile ring in the Vatican, what would Jesus say?
Why do Black people get emotional
over the description
of Jesus dying on a cross
but not from Black men
still hanging from trees?
We've gone from
pyramids to plantations to projects to prisons
standing on the edge of tomorrow
not making good decisions
not realizing that
they're killing democracy softly
we are the ones we've been waiting for
and as we fiddle while Rome burns
the world thinks we're suckers
wondering WTF
waiting on you to fit in
where you can fit in
and pick up
whatever you can pick up
meantime
we suffer from a lack of knowledge
distracted with bullshit
like running Oprah for President
when we should be finding a way to talk about impeaching POTUS
and ending the Electoral College,
how about our civil rights got short circuited?

We need to fight for self determination
in fact make this go viral
a luta continua
the struggle still continues for liberation.

## On the Day the Pope Died

On the Day the Pope died
no one knew that he'd been dead
since before 9/11
no one told you,
no one paid enough attention
to push him over
obviously not crusaders praying to Jesus
while bombing mosques
they say he was a man of peace
admonished by St Lauryn Hill
for the sins of pedophile priest
gas prices rising like the flames of souls
dying for oil and the lies about those
weapons of mass destruction yet to be found
tsunami's rage like the tears of the planet
wounded and ravaged by a raped ecology
as water becomes the next commodity
it wasn't on the Disney channel
so don't look on FOX 5 or HOT 97
where misled hip hoppers pimp Coca-Cola
and labor leaders disappear from Colombia
where the peso is worth even less than the dollar
did the evangelicals tell you in church on Sunday
that social security has been hi-jacked by gangsters
the Christians that lied and stole two elections?
So on the day the pope died
the most impoverished people in the land
who are mostly black, beige, and brown
still genuflect to a white man
heads bowed kneeling on the ground
giving their hard-earned cash
to the richest men on earth
while the kingdom of heaven is within
so on the day the Pope died

the truly faithful cried and gave praise to
Mary, the Black Madonna, otherwise known as Isis
marched in the street bearing death symbols
turned their backs to the Vatican
for not excommunicating Hitler
opened their closets and burned sage
to exorcise demons
set fire to fascist disguised as Republicans
fanned the coals while channeling Phoenix
on the day the Pope died
El Salvadoran martyrs were still not vindicated
Archbishop Romero turned in his grave
as the death of Sister Dorothy Stang of Brazil
is being investigated and the conspiracy of murder
continues against peasants protecting the rain forest
angels of justice guard brave priests like Rev Leclerc
and Sandoval
as they preach the theology of liberation
in a land that is evil and hostile
so on the day the Pope died
it seemed as if no one had been listening
as millions of oppressed nationalities
left the earth from man-made dis-eases
while coat hangers return for those seeking abortions
still Mumia Abu Jamal sits on death row
and our children suffer death from McDonalds
trying to pay back student loans with salaries from
Starbucks
dreaming of making a living on Def Jam
combing the country doing open mics and poetry
slams
til realizing the dream's turned into a nightmare
as Def Jam poets line up for welfare
so on the day the Pope died
we pray for a new regime
that truly reflects a culture of life

where the strong will truly protect the weak
as bells ring in the Vatican
sending vibrations throughout the planet
for the true liberation of the human spirit.

## Uncomfortable Conversations

Many times Black folk
go out of their way not to make white folk
feel uncomfortable
but we've been uncomfortable
ever since we were brought here in chains
when driving while Black
every time we hear a police siren
we live in fear
living in a police state
but you say
it can't happen here
in these yet to be United States
that you claim is post-racial
but these cops act like having brown skin is illegal
living in a reality show where there is no sequel
when we go into a department store
you follow us like thieves
but we're the ones that were stolen
along with whole countries
along with our history that's outlawed and aborted
our story distorted
Ausar, Auset, and Heru
replaced by blue-eyed Jesus
then led to believe that anything unchristian is a sin
and that there was no history
before the Nicaean Council 325 A.D.
or around 1611 when that perverted James the King
rewrote the Bible that he stole
from The Egyptian Book of the Dead it's been said
The Sun Book a.k.a. The Book of Coming Forth by Day
extracting the 42 Laws of Ma'at
and leaving only 10 Commandments

you would need to read more books to understand this
but media and gangsta rap makes education unpopular these days
so intellectual curiosity has taken a backstage
to video games
hand to eye coordination
training folk to be quick on the trigger
for wars never ending
the economy is broken
so to foreign lands your sons and daughters they are sending
to maim, kill, and murder those who pray to Allah
meanwhile social media overloads of distraction
inundating us with commercials, got us trying to keep up with the joneses
while children in China slave in sweatshops making smartphones
broken windows/stop and frisk policy
is a part of the conspiracy
the criminalization of a generation
in a country where the rate of incarceration
is the largest in the (I wish I could call it) civilized world
and whole cities are employed from prison privatization
as a means to control population
where the demographic is rapidly changing
from White to Black and Brown
meanwhile there's still a struggle concerning abortion
cancer treatment has become an industry
cause in the cure there's no profit
the educational system is only designed for training
critical thought is lacking
they don't want us thinking
we just might figure out fascism is rising

so we need to have these uncomfortable
conversations
it's too late to change the channel
the atmosphere is polluted with radiation and it's not
safe
to put your head in the sand
now we're doing die ins
chanting
"Hands Up! Don't Shoot!" or
"I Can't Breathe!"

## I'm in a Recovery Program from Western Civilization

Epigraph:

Recent statistics reveal that two out of every three Black males between the ages of 20 and 29 are incarcerated, on parole, or on probation. This poem is livicated to them.

Once they gave me that Social Security number
I knew how Jews felt in Auschwitz
I wasn't even asked
"Here," they said, "You're a citizen,"
pay us, vote for us
call it democracy or starve
punch the clock
all worth is by the hour
time is gold
and he who defines wins
the unemployment lines grow faster
than cancer on a prostate
the welfare line is shorter than no paycheck
life gets uglier than a boil on a redneck's neck
the talk shows blame everything
on the economically disadvantaged
the mayor says move if you can't find a job
fascism rises like a silent fart, quiet but deadly
kneegrows act like ostriches
panhandling is illegal
city hall fans the flames on the battlefield of race
but whatever happened to government for all the people
and did you vote to lose your job

does repression really breed resistance or is this some mad fantasy
all I know is the fat cats got their hooks in me
and I sure wish a million Black men in atonement on the White House lawn
had done much more than trample the grass
especially in Washington, the District of Columbia
the last plantation, an apartheid colony in this US of A
where the citizens have no vote
and by-the-way South Africa
now that you can mark x on the ballot, can you spend it?
Can you take it to the bank where the krugerrand rules
and is worth much more than a U.S. dollar bill?
And did you get your fill and did you get your land back?
Does democracy really hold the keys to freedom?
She's incarcerated in the criminal injustice system
a very criminal system of justice
she's sitting in a $125,000 dollar cell
on death row with life without parole
you know freedom she's stamping out license plates and sewing blue jeans
breaking rocks on an Alabama chain gang for 3 cents a day
got a master's degree in economics
and is doing life for being the truth
damn does it seem like slavery's in style again?
What a brotha know
there are no more doors
for spooks to sit by.

## Anatomy of a Lynching (Contemporary Sketches of Amerikkka)

Bloody Monday
June 8, 1998
phone rings two minutes before my alarm
the usual sexy voice on the end of my phone
frantically sez
"Didn't you listen to the news?
Didn't you hear about Jasper, Texas?
A Black Man, James Byrd Jr.
beaten and dragged
from the back of a truck!"
"Damn, that's a hell of a way you've got
for waking up a brother," I sez,
one of them had white supremacist tattoos
and was talking trash about the Turner Diaries
claim they found my man's body parts
along the road for two miles
when the truck stopped he was headless
must be that Jack Daniels and Budweiser
redneck's piss
you know they go crazy when they drink that shit
start killing their mamas, raping their daughters,
barking at the moon,
setting examples for their kids
the Black mayor and his cronies
claim they didn't know about
any white supremacist in the area
and that it was an isolated tragedy
I spoze that's why brotha man's the mayor
cause he don't know about secret societies
so secret they're on the Internet
maybe Jasper, Texas didn't get that yet
local citizens say
racism is as much of Jasper as death

the cracka that killed him had a favorite hymn
"Take My Hand, Precious Lord"
spoze God told him to do it
Scriptures say strange shit
when read thru the bottom of a bottle
damn
you got a helluva way
of waking up a brother,
can we start again
"Good Morning. I Love You."

## Countdown Y2K

I carry my bombs in notebooks
I can't afford a plane
you say I'm a word terrorist
because I record secrets in the palms of my hands
I throw word bombs from stages
creating a barrage on your mind
for the mind is the last frontier
so I'm a neo-cerebral pioneer
it's 1998 almost '99
lines at ATM machines wrap around the planet
the rush is on before all systems go back to zero
you betta act like you know
Mother Earth's pissed
hot enough to melt polar ice caps
causing floods to wash away transgressors
God sez she's no longer listening to bullshit
rays darting from her eyes setting fire to dogma
true believers piss on temples
trying to put out the flames
hi-jackings on bicycles are frequent
and there's no computer to translate the Bible code
so everythang's up for grabs
there's a sale on survival kits
but the cash registers don't work
all the clocks punched out
the moon is dripping blood as a million Muslims
say "Salat!" at midnight
the clock tick tocks racing to see if time stops
prisoners of the night, those who do time
but don't believe in it, breakdance til dawn,
smelling freedom at daybreak
workers never united have no jobs to go to
gold is not edible and you can't drink oil
the sun has scorched a hole in the ozone

race is no longer relevant
everyone's scorched charcoal
poets and prophets broadcast the news from street
corners
while flying kites in thunderstorms
trying to recapture electricity
the monthly Metro card you bought last night
no longer works
the cops are dressed in riot gear
waiting for you to jump the turnstile
seems like you'll miss that appointment
at the beauty parlor for your date tonight
hope it's by candlelight
and you're not depending on the microwave
to cook dinner
churches still pass the offering plate
praying that the streets of heaven
are paved with gold like they've been told
it's raining airplanes
you'd better duck quick
there's no television to broadcast revolution
third eye blindness distorts inner visions
there'll be no government to make decisions
you'll have to do it for yourself
as automatic coffee pots go berserk
and you finally wake up and realize
that dumb shit like who's sucking the president's dick
is not so damn important anymore.

## Poem For The Absent Minded

There's some rumbling in the air
that says you just don't care
saying you just think we should forget about it
living in a killture of selective amnesia
but I'm not trying to forget
maybe that's why I was sent
to jar your memory
hoping that the truth will set you free
after all we weren't slaves before they brought us here
planting seeds of fear
using the Bible, the Lash, and the Gun
erasing the memory of where we've come from
flipping scripts so you won't know about
Ausar, Auset, and Heru
the original trinity
distorting us with His Story
instead of truth
that's why I remind you
of Sojourner,
Nanny and Nzingha,
Nat and Tshaka Zulu,
Fannie Lou and Tubman, too,
now they're turning in their graves
cause in this modern-day society
not much has changed
as we're fooled
chains removed from arms and legs
but wrapped around your brain
in denial of the matrix
see I remember Civil Rights,
I remember when we stood up to fight,
I remember Black Power and

Black Panthers with shot guns on the courthouse steps,
I remember Imamu Amiri Baraka and Simba Wachanga, too,
that's why I write these poems to you
I remember Black fists held high
for each Black man's eulogy a pig would die
violence is as Amerikkkan as apple pie
quoting H. Rap Brown
a.k.a. Jamil Abdulla Al-Amin now in Super Max
I remember Watts and Newark, too,
BLA, Assata,
and New Afrikan Freedom Fighters
who fought for me and you,
I recall George and Jonathan Jackson,
I write this poem for Fred Hampton
murdered while sleeping in his bed
Chicago Pigs filled him full of lead,
I remember Geronimo Pratt,
now let's get down to the bare facts
Amerikkka is in denial that there are
Black Freedom Fighters here
but there are at least 69
and I'm not talking sex
there's plenty of reasons to be vexed
no telling who they'll lock up next
I'm not talking about your everyday criminal
but those who made a conscious choice
to stand and fight or framed by the viciousness of COINTELPRO
chained up locked down
never seeing daylight
some in solitary confinement 40 years or more
no contact with the outside world
nor human touch
locked away longer than Mandela,

locked away longer than those convicted
of the laws called Rockefeller
I remember when Illadelphia's no good Goode
moved on John Afrika and the MOVE Family
see a lot of you have forgotten
about Mumia Abu Jamal
but he's only one of many
standing tall behind the wall
Like Oscar Lopez Rivera, Ruchell Magee,
Sekou Odinga, Russell Maroon Shoatz,
the Angola Three,
Lynne Stewart, Mutulu Shakur,
Jalil Muntaqim, Leonard Peltier,
Herman Wallace and Abdul Majid,
just some of the New African Warriors captured
that need to be freed
so now you've been informed
since you've heard some of the facts
I'm giving you the contacts
here's what we can do..

Contact: The Jericho Movement

JerichoNY.org

## One Last Poem for Amiri B

Dawta hit me with the text
saying Amiri B had left the building
I'm still tryin ta find words to express my funk
the pain was like having teeth ripped out with no anesthesia
leaving a hole that has no filling
Amiri was like another father to me
he named me Ngoma back in '71
I been trying to live up to the attribute ever since
there's a pledge we took that's still tattooed to my consciousness
"We are sworn African Revolutionaries!
We will make revolution or die!"
I've been soldiering since then
he taught us that culture is a weapon
so I stay strapped
fully loaded slinging stones at Goliath
swinging my axe tryin ta knock down the walls of Jericho
but this poem ain't about me
this poem is about the master teacher
the legacy he left and the record that he set
it's about recognizing the fact
that the truth will set you free
so the fact remains we're still at war
and the battle ain't over
to see the way forward
remember the concept of Sankofa
go back to your old-time religions
return to your ancestors' visions
go to the crossroads and pray
for Elegba to open the way
just don't forget freedom ain't free
and Kazi (Work) is the Blackest of all

I realize this poem is sloganized,
plagiarized, and cliche
but the last thing that I want to say
is don't mourn, organize.

## Don't Call Me No Poet (This Ain't No Love Song)

Mama taught me that prayer changes things
so I'm prayin' for enough steel to keep it real
cause death is the only door out of here
but we be scared to leave our bodies
this body's been kicked around long enough
it wasn't spozed to last forever
and my soul cries out to be free
besides the only thing constant is change
so I'm sittin' meditating on the one
when a B Boy with a Boom Box
scared my spirit guides away
and I'm lost in a rat race
tryin ta buy shit my TV sez I need to survive
and I'm searching for freedom
but I can't define it anymore
so I'm on a vision quest
tryin ta find a way out of this mess
walking thru the park talking to the trees
they've got a protest going on
against giving up their lives for Cashmas
and the local snowmakers union
refuses to cross the picket line
'til Santa kicks in with a kick back
so it's 75 degrees in New York in December
seems like the whole damn universe is under attack
by the greedy as they plunder the world
exploiting the needy
so I'm rolling seven ankhs deep in mysticism
meditated til the lights went out
but Con Ed wasn't hearing it
not even an ohm could cut the darkness
so I'm burning seven candles
tryin ta find the light of God inside
but she's busy down at the Salvation Army

healing the bell ringer who was shot
by a 10 yearly white kid with a Tec-9 from Oregon
seems like faith was raped of her charity
and everything seems hopeless
so I'm hanging out in poetry circles
searching for the truth
but all I get is soft porn stroking my ego
to erection with no satisfaction
too many poets saying nothing well
but I'm lookin' for substance
something I can take home
there's not enough meat for a doggie bag
so I stick to vegetarianism like a religion
tryin ta ward off starvation
I'm chanting for peace and justice
but Kenneth Banks was murdered
by the new weapon of choice
a killa kop's two-way radio to the head
killed him dead
no back up needed,
no caution heeded,
now I'm praying for Buddha
he's lying face down spread eagle on the concrete
jacked up by 5-O on the corner of 112th St
and the interest on karmic debt is higher than bail
seems like he'll do Cashmas in jail
the herb spots been shut down
to improve the quality of life
for street corner pharmaceuticals who offer
death at half the price
while the last legal drug dealer
aka local watering holes like the News Room in the Bronx
offers three for one shots of rot gut watered down
except for poets like me ,banned for using the n word,
cause the owner is an n word

but alcoholism kills the liver first
and it's easy to collect from the taxes of the dead
so I scream other obscenities instead like
poverty plus ignorance plus imperialism equals fascism
but justice turns a deaf ear to my fears
so I'm looking for a detox for Jesus addiction
but the offering plate gets in the way
cause organized religion is big business
but nobody tells the poor
as they pay and pray for more salvation
from this hell we're living in
so Hail Mary full of gold the Vatican's
been bought and sold
remember we had homes and jobs
before they brought us here
my ancestors built pyramids for years
before picking cotton
maybe that's been forgotten
now I'm quotin Haki Madhubuti
"Jesus Saves, Jesus Saves, Jesus Saves
Green stamps"
But Green stamps are obsolete
while the poor and the homeless beg for food to eat
in this land of plenty where not a damn thing is free
so don't call me a poet
cause me
I'm just a pissed off brother with a pen.

# ***The Corona Chronicles***

## The Hood Greets Rona

Pour a little liquor
for the new ancestors
we ain't scared of no virus
it's the cops that be killin us
we still guard bodegas on the corner
masks are made for stick up
Big Pharma wanna
stick up the world
selling vaccines copyrighted in 2015
for man-made catastrophe
like we don't know disaster
when we smell it
we read Behold a Pale Horse
you can fool some of the people some time
but you can't fool all the people
all the time
game peeped game
we remember Tuskegee
poisoned blankets and the Trail of Tears
it's no secret
Bill Gates, Trump, and the Rothschilds
got Fourth Reich on the brain
bought stock in 5G and microchips
but all of us ain't sleep
we post the truth on Facebook
instead of fake news on your tel-a-lie vision
does genocide meet the community standard,
maybe reality has been quarantined?

## Said I Wasn't Gonna Talk About Death

Said I wasn't gonna talk about death
after all
it's only the other side of life
why can't we applaud survival,
after all everybody hasn't
died (at least not yet)?
How about those who lived
to tell the stories about
how disease did not kill them
I'll bet there are more of them
I guess it's too good for fake news
or predictions without divination
by politricktians
instead of scientists
about something that
never happened before
but there's no profit in that
it doesn't sell masks, respirators,
or body bags
doesn't usher in the new world order
said I wasn't going to
talk about death
mostly because I believe in spirits
but not in ghosts
we have conversations on the regular
they say "Don't be afraid
for life has no beginning and no end
only energy changing
from one thing to other things."
I said I wasn't going to
talk about death
fear not
it's only the other side of life.

## Fear of a Black Planet

Here in the wild wild west
that thinks Islam is the enemy
it's funny how everyone is masked
like orthodox habiba's
and Behold a Pale Horse
becomes a book of prophecy
chemical warfare is the order of the day
obviously heroin, crack, cocaine, opiods, and killer kops
didn't do the job fast enough
so stock market crashes
bring enforced microchip inoculation
as media indoctrination rules.
Fear of a Black planet
got white supremacist shaking in their boots
with the realization that we are
oppressed nationalities
not minorities
so the whole damn world's on lockdown
hoping people of color
stay six feet a part
and stop producing babies
making those with melanin deficiencies
obsolete.

## Mother Nature Has No Cashapp

So now that a stay-at-home order
is in full effect
what do the homeless do?
File for unemployment benefits
from the job they never had?
How can they be counted for the census?
Where is the bailout
for those who did not have
taxes to file for nonexistent work
and have no bank account
for direct deposit?
Since meat packing plants are contaminated
will we all be vegetarians?
Wouldn't that make everyone healthier?
Will there be a civil war
waged by redneck 45 followers
protesting against stay-at-home laws
refusing to wear face masks?
Will they all die from sharing air space
as they rage against the machine
and suffer a mass burial?
Maybe we'll be better off without them.
Will the earth become fertilized
with the carcasses of the dispossessed?
Will flowers of peace and justice
bloom in the springtime?
Who will repay the loan of stimulus checks?
How can there be retribution?
Mother nature has no cashapp.

## Masks (What Will Be Will Be)

So
what do you think
now that the world
has no face
just the invisibility of fear?
So beaches and
liquor stores on corners are open
as we look death in the eye
tauntingly seeking answers to
the cycles of life and death
knowing damn well that
one can't exist without the other.
Is Mother Nature purging
or have conspiracy theories
come full circle karmic debt on steroids?
After all when climate champions
sounded the alarm
those in denial turned a deaf ear
though streets flooded
and forest fires raged
dolphins washed up on shores
and polar bears lost their habitat
now each day is like Groundhog Day
out of touch with touch
reality is virtual
with no sense of taste or smell
growing fat from boredom and home cooking
stir crazy
45'ers drink Lysol and disinfectant
while we wonder
if they're too dumb to read the label
so much for the miseducation shitstem
but for some of us
homeschooling is a favor

though everyone misses
contact with their friends
no high fives at sport events
but just think
of all the souls reincarnating
a universe striving balance
just remember
what will be will be.

## This Plandemic Ain't New

About 1492
it landed in the Bahamas
thinking it was India
things been jacked up since then
trading beads and Bibles for land
on the trail of broken treaties
racism is the thesis
but these school of life dropouts
just don't get it
so killer bees
or killer kops
death hangs out in the shadows
waiting for the eagle to fall
and there's
not enough social distancing
to take back stolen land
so heart drum beats
from Atlanta to Auschwitz,
from Tuskegee to Mississippi
to Palestine
and there's no justice in the hood
but a bullseye
on a jogger's back
for running while Black
going to church could
get you killed as we pray
to Jesus to save us
from this disaster of a virus
that the resident in the White House
who obviously cut science class
and has always been absent from church
says it's safe
since obviously
he won't be there.

## SOS on the Nu Titanic

Trumpleskinthin
champion nose grower
in contest with Pinocchio
cloud follow him
like Joe Btfsplk
in Lil Abner
captives jump ship
like new slaves
blindfolded by reality
Google idiot
his face appear in multiples
ego playing chicken
with Cashmas payroll
stick up kid
with no gun
demands six billion for a wall
kickbacks guaranteed
the kingdom is for sale to the highest bidder
gentrification in the White's house
in the middle of Chocolate City
et tu, Brute?
dominoes falling like a house of cards
pressure soon burst
like a water pipe
force of the empire
20,000 strong
back home from Syria
to guard the wall
along the border
in this alternate reality
governed on Twitter
airplanes don't exist
in a universe of
I told you so

the prophet asks
"Will you listen to the writing
on the walls of your consciousness
this time?"

## 20/20

It don't take
20/20 vision
to hear
I can't breathe again
just when you thought
it was safe to breathe while Black
we can't outrun the reality
that we are under attack
from COVID-19 and
the rise of the Ku Klux Klan again
trying to make America great
though it never was more
than a refuge for colonizers
a failed experiment
like Frankenstein
in the age of 5G
where war shape shifts daily
and newspeak has the
mind boggled illiterates
not knowing what to believe
or what to read
since literacy is out of style
in the land of gadgets
and everyone is out of touch
masked to the fact that
social media and the five o'clock blues
all owned by the same tycoons
never promised you the truth
or a rose garden
and all the news could be fake anyway
only the shadow knows for sure.

## Breakin' News

Here
in the yet to be United States
bereavement hangs like a cloud
leftover from the storm
of antebellum attitudes
omitted from his story books
so the melanin deficient
never learned about Sankofa
or the Emancipation Proclamation
and it's open season
on the melanated
and it seems like the combination
when a killer kop is guilty
is three nights of riot equals one kop arrested
but there are three more to go
and looters can be shot on sight
without rights of a constitution extinct
in a state of emergency
and everyone can see
the emperor has no clothes
and there's fyah
burnin in the streets of
Babylon.

## The Scream of Silence

There's a subtle scream of silence
permeating the air
from the pulpit of those
that wave the stars and bars
and scowl behind the Holy Babble
that was never read
threatening to defy the constitution
sending the military
to fight those who come in peace
to mourn the death of civility
hoping to bury Jim Crow
planting flowers of peace and justice
on the grave
but there are low flying choppers
hovering over the White's House
sweatin' strange conversations
in the bunker in the basement
and a new wall being built
in Chocolate City (not Mexico)
as the offsprings of the rainbow
shine their light into the darkness
soldiers and policeman take a knee
but like my brothers and sisters in Missouri
SHOW ME
cause the slave catchers
evolved to killer kops
we defy curfews and plandemics
with our hands in the air
children of the rainbow
surround the planet
like a group hug
but don't forget
we've had these Kumbaya moments before
will it be different this time?

## Things Fall Apart

All the king's horses
and all the king's men
couldn't put Humpty
together again
is more than a nursery rhyme
I thought it was a dream
until waking up to the reality
that things are falling apart
it seems there's an alternative universe
as Amerikkka implodes on itself
excuse me but
I told you so seems appropriate
as predictions shift into reality
there's 25,000 troops
camped on the White House lawn
but how do we know
if they're all on the same page?
Or if it's true that militias, kops, and klan
go hand in hand
after all somebody knew
there's a maze underneath the capital
it was known that the Magaz were coming
but no one was called for help
so I'd say there's something rotten
and this ain't Denmark
could this be karma
or is this the newest banana republic?
Is this the beginning
of a civil war
or will the earth open up
and swallow the Philistines
that came to hang the Congress?
After all, this all started with Lincoln
so it sure won't go away with impeachment

the termites are out of the woodwork
and Jim Crow is in style again.

## In the Absence of Ka-Ching

The vaccination indoctrination
all in the name of cash
but cash may soon be useless
it could spread the virus
now, what do I do with paper,
no plastic do I own?
Besides, plastic's now illegal
what will beggars beg for when
no exchange is done with change?
Now no one has a face,
eyeballs scanned at airports
masked robber barons
sell enforced inoculations
experiment on the dispossessed.
Poe said
The ravens cry nevermore

## Aftermath

I'm accepting contributions
from all the rednecks who want to
send me back to Africa
and also I'm contributing
to the fund
to send you back to caves
in fact
since things seem to have come full circle
I hope some of my liberal white friends
will buy me back again
realize though
we're not our great-great grandparents
we're reincarnated and evolved Egun
and we will fuck you up
we've been practicing
taking lessons from the
dog eat dog example
of crabs in the barrel
realize too
that some of us read
and we ain't going for the same lies and bullshit
I watch FOX News
Massa's house is on fyah
tell the field niggas to hurry up and fan the flames
political correctness flew out the window
escaped like a runaway slave
and apologies for protesting
just seem absent from my vocabulary
since the system showed
that the government don't
give a damn about Black people
get your alcohol and cotton balls
this pimple called America
on the butt cheek of the world is about to burst

caught with your pants down
sodomized with no grease
didn't get kissed first
and feelings are hurt
bitchin 'bout Democrats vs Republicans
hope you finally learned that
we must do for self.

## The Real Amerikkka

The real Amerikkka
showed up and showed out
and we ask
where's a cop with u need one
it wasn't no secret
that the Magaz was coming
it was all on social media
maybe the National Guard didn't come
cause the Black female mayor called them
see where I'm going here.
They showed up for Black Lives Matter
brought tanks on the Ave
but then again
who would have thought T-Rump
would instigate a take over
the question is
how many impeachments does it take
to get rid of a lunatic
and what's taking so long?
But then again
I hope u weren't surprised
after all
this is the real Amerikkka
built on stolen Indian land
and the backs of Africans
the whole damned thing is a lie
drunk on the blood of Manifest Destiny
so don't act like
shit didn't always stink
been funked up
since Columbus got lost.

# The House Is on Fyah

So i be fannin flames
I got no tears left
there's a knee, a choke hold,
41 shots, a plunger,
a hangman's noose, and
a new lunch hour blues
death repeatedly comes
in circles like a hamster's wheel
over and over
and it's past time for it to stop
as there are tanks
on the boulevards of Amerikkka
police cars on fire
it's 2020 and 20 fake dollars
and a knee on the neck of democracy
plus a Plandemic got the world
in the streets
when the politrictans say there's no profit
in a lockdown
so we gamble with death
until the forced vaccination is ready
everybody will be glad to take it
but I remember Jonestown,
Dachau, Tuskegee,
Rwanda, and the Trail of Tears
I know what genocide looks like
so don't think
I'm not happy to see y'all
but this conversation
been going on since 1619
where the hell you been anyhow
i guess a few weeks of burnin and lootin
finally got your attention
but we need much more than

the US Congress taking a knee
wearing Kente
although it's now a part of the pageant
and everybody's got a role to play
we're riding this freedom train
til the wheels fall off
so get in where you fit in
cause there'll be no peace without Justice
the resident in the White's House
is hiding out in a bunker in the basement
building walls in Chocolate City
not Mexico
as we stand at the crossroads
begging Elegba not to trick us
as we pray for Ogun with his machete
and Oya to blow the winds of change.

## Pestilence

This ain't the first pestilence
the Holy Babble even gave warning
it may not be the last
it's another chapter
payment of karmic debt
a time to look at all the history
you want me to forget
but the statues of Confederacy
are still standing on my chest
and the knee of killer kops
remain on my neck
and I'm trying to figure out
why we ain't figured out
that we're standing at the
crossroad
at the intersection of Corona Boulevard,
Gun Avenue, and Killa Kops?
So tell Becky don't throw a Karen
the pimple of poverty is about to burst
and it's gonna take more than skin cream
this acne been building
since the Good Ship Jesus
everything is everything
and all things are connected
seems like the septic tank of life
is backed up
while the resident in the White's House
continues to play golf
in some altered state of reality
blind to the fact that
the truth in bold yellow letters
has been painted on the avenue
of his luxury building
telling the whole damned world that

Black Lives Matter
and the moving van is waiting at the door.

# Pass/Past/Puff

The ancestors crowded the kitchen
knocking food on to the floor
eating before their red cracked plate
could be piled high with food and served
from ancient recipes in DNA
passed down from mouth to ear
water flooded the floor
Osun made her presence known
pounded yam, snail, and Egusi stew
prepared
Osala accepts these prayers and offerings
on this ninth trip around the sun
I'm having trouble remembering what day it is
blame it on COVID
everyone is masked or quarantined
it seems like Groundhog Day
last week disappeared
I didn't know it was gone
it's a bit disturbing
when I can count the number
of my friends that are still on the planet
on 10 fingers
the world is at my fingertips
but I miss the feel of earth between my toes
though I'm a city dweller
I lived on hill sides many lives ago
years create some foolish thought
that time can be measured
it's only a mirage spawned by mortals
but who is to say what is real
or how long it takes to build a pyramid
when all existence is immediate
and pass/present/future is synonymous.

She came singing
happy rebirth of the Sun
thru the manger of Capricorn
not the son, Son,
the planets still rotate
only change is constant
all the news got me buying stock in bodybags
how do I know if the vaccine is not more deadly
than the dis-ease?
Will there be a COVID shot police
and a prison cell for those who refuse
to be human lab rats?
So we stand on the edge
of a new decade
and all of the passwords say
EXPIRED.

# Artist's Statement

I am a modern-day griot and multi-instrumentalist who practices his art through the use of poetry, song, and music. My work is specifically crafted to raise social, political, and spiritual consciousness through social critique and commentary using these artistic mediums. I create and use music that invokes the richness of our history as a reference point. I accomplish this through the use of slave, work freedom, jazz, blues, traditional African spiritual, and folk songs. My obsession and love of music has led me to play several instruments: violin, bamboo flute, yidaki (erroneously called the didgeridoo), guitar, and assorted percussion instruments that in West African griot tradition provide an engaging platform for my original poems. I continue faithfully in this tradition by addressing a myriad of topics that include social and environmental justice, women's rights, peace and nuclear disarmament, prisoner's rights, voting rights and economic inequities. I connect the dots to show how these entities are connected. I enjoy performing solo or with an ensemble and often collaborate with other artists both in performance and recording.

I have been an activist since my senior year in high school during the Civil Rights era and throughout my adult life. I am intentional in my efforts and I make sure that my work is informative and thought provoking. I am an avid reader and researcher and as such, I integrate the information that I gather in my presentations to educate and bring a fresh perspective from the past to the present. I endeavor and hope to influence what could happen in the future.

My work spans fifty years and has been presented in venues that include private and public-school classes, assemblies, colleges, universities, community centers, rallies as large as the largest anti-nuclear rally in Central Park for a million people, several union labor rallies in the Madison Square Garden performance complex, as well as prisons, churches, nightclubs, social clubs, coffee houses, concert stages, subways, and street corners. I have been known to perform my craft wherever working people struggle for a better life.

# Biography

**Ngoma** is a performance poet, multi-instrumentalist, singer, songwriter and paradigm shifter who has used culture as a tool to raise socio-political and spiritual consciousness through work that encourages critical thought. A former member of Amiri Baraka's The Spirit House Movers and Players and the contemporary freedom song duo Serious Bizness, Ngoma weaves poetry and song that raises contradictions and searches for a solution to a just and peaceful world. Ngoma was the Prop Slam Winner of the 1997 National Poetry Slam Competition in Middletown, CT and his been published in African Voices Magazine, Long Shot Anthology, The Underwood Review, Signifyin' Harlem Review, Bum Rush the Page/Def Poetry Jam Anthology, Poems on the Road to Peace -(Volumes 1, 2, and 3) Yale Press, Let Loose On the World-Amiri Baraka at 75, The Understanding Between Foxes and Light - Great Weather For Media, New Rain-Blind Beggar Press 35th Anniversary Issue. He was featured in the PBS spoken word documentary The Apropoets with Allen Ginsburg.

Ngoma has curated and hosted the poetry slam at the Martin Luther King Family Festival of Social and Environmental Justice at the Yale/Peabody Museum since 1995. He was also selected to participate in the 2009 Badilisha Poetry Xchange in Capetown, South Africa. In December of 2011 He was initiated as a Priest of Obatala in Ibadan, Nigeria. In June of 2013 he was initiated as a Priest of Ifa.

On his latest CD Conversation with Esu, Ngoma serves up another helping of smokin' spoken word with jazz/funk/fusion and a slice or two of world beat. Electric Violin, Yidaki a.k.a Didgeridoo, and Garage Band tracks serve as a platform for his political and spiritual conscious raising lyrics along with his vocalizing a song or two to sweeten your palate and feed your mind. Known for controversy, this CD will not disappoint as the newly initiated Ifa Priest invokes Orishas and Eguns to join the party with enough funk to put a hump in your back.

## CD Reviews

"Ngoma is a living sage amongst those who do not have the courage to see their greater selves. His poetry is profound, poignant, and necessary at a time like this or any other. This CD should be listened to with understanding. It is not traditional but it is our tradition. Once again in the midst of madness sanity creeps through to remind us all is not lost and if we chose to we have the power to make a better day."

- Abiodun Oyewole of the Last Poets


"Ngoma Hill is one of my faves on the NYC spoken word scene. His words - beautifully crafted, infused with wisdom, packing a wallop of a punch. He also has some of the best pipes on the planet. My advice to young guns in spoken word: Listen to his new CD, Poetry From A Smart Phone. See the art form done at its best. Stripped of ego and BS, but someone with something to say & looking to make a difference."

Michael Gefner - Producer and Curator/The Inspired Word-NYC

**Services Provided**

Performance Poetry - 15 min Set

Performance Poetry with Music

Performance with Band

Performance Poetry Concert with Band

<u>Host-</u>

Poetry Slam or Poetry Event


Workshops

Use of Music with Performance Poetry

Poetry as a Tool for Social Change


<u>Lectures</u>

Music and Poetry: The Culture of Resistance


<u>Sound Healing</u>

Sound Healing with Reiki

Reiki

## Studio Work

Create instrumental music as background for poet recordings

Places

Southern Connecticut State University

Yale University

Three Rivers Community College

Quinipiac University

Ryder University

Columbia University

Medgar Evers College

C.C.N.Y

Hunter College

Rutgers U (New Brunswick)*

Marshall U.  * W.Va

_____

## Some of the Artist that I have shared stages with

Amiri Baraka
Sonia Sanchez
Saul Williams
Roger Bonair Agard
Jessica Care Moore
Mumz da Schemer
Mike Ladd
Darian Dachaun
The Welfare Poets
Odetta
Pete Seeger
Chaka Khan
Sweet Honey in the Rock
Jackson Brown
Richie Havens
Linton Kwesi Johnson
Mutabaruka
The Persuasions

## Some of the Places I've Been

INTERNATIONAL VENUES

Queen Elizabeth Hall (London, England)

Theatre Noir - (Paris, France )

The Shanghai Conservatory of Music -Shanghai, China (Lecture Demonstration)

The Badilisha Poetry Xchange - (Cape Town, South Africa (Workshops and Concerts)

Street Theater - (Bonn, Germany)
**Local Venues-**

Central Park, NYC *

Madison Square Garden *

The Felt Forum *

Symphony Hall*  Newark, NJ

Symphony Space - NYC *

The Nuyorican Poets Cafe  NYC

The Apollo -NYC


S.O.B's-NYC

Folk City -NYC

## Discography

Echoes of Prayer - Grachan Moncur
Juju Chapter II - Nia - Plunky and Oneness of Juju
Serious Bizness:For Your Immediate Attention - Folkways
Serious Bizness:How Many More- Folkways
Brown Butterfly-Craig Harris
Ngoma:Paradigm Shifin'
Ngoma's Take Out
Ngoma:Poetry From a Smart Phone
Lessons From the Book of Osayemi
Lessons from the Book of Osayemi (Chapter II)
Conversation with Esu
Music For My Soldiers

## Theater

In White America - Folk Singer - Va. State University
Junkies Are Full of Shit - Big Time - The Spirit House Movers and Players-Amiri
What's the Relationship of the Lone Ranger to the Means of Production- Amiri Baraka
The River Niger - Mo- The Barksdale Theater- Richmond, VA
A History of the Universe According to Those Who Have to Live in It- University of the Street - NYC

## Ngoma
*Performance Poet/Multi-Instrumentalist*

Contact and Booking Information
**Ngomazworld@aol.com**
(646)228-6841

www.ingramcontent.com/pod-product-compliance
Lightning Source LLC
Chambersburg PA
CBHW071313110426
42743CB00042B/1485